ISAIAH & JEREMIAH

A SELF-STUDY GUIDE

Irving L. Jensen

MOODY PRESS

CHICAGO

ISBN: 0-8024-4464-4

1 2 3 4 5 6 7 Printing/EP/Year 94 93 92 91 90

Printed in the United States of America

Contents

Introduction   4

PROPHETS IN GENERAL

1. The Audience of the Prophets   5
2. The Prophets of God   18

ISAIAH

3. The Man Isaiah   27
4. The Book of Isaiah   36
5. Isaiah's Vision of Judah   44
6. Isaiah's Call and Commission   51
7. The Suffering Servant   58

JEREMIAH

8. The Man Jeremiah   65
9. The Book of Jeremiah   77
10. Jeremiah's Call and Commission   86
11. The Parable of the Potter   92

LAMENTATIONS

12. The Book of Lamentations   97
    Geography of Isaiah and Jeremiah   101
    Kings of Israel   102
    Kings of Judah   103
    Chart of Kings and Prophets   104
    Bibliography   106

Introduction

Study of the prophetical books of the Bible can be a stimulating experience to the one who pursues it with care and zeal. Often these books are neglected on the false assumption that they are altogether too difficult, overly technical, and even uninteresting. Those who study them know better. The messages of the prophets could not be more timely, partly because we are living in the last days, of which the books prophesy, and partly because the religious and political conditions of the world today are much like those of the prophets' days.

The main reason that a book of prophecy may be difficult to understand is that the person reading it is not acquainted with the various aspects of the background of the book, such as its historical setting. It is with this in mind that the first two lessons of this manual are devoted to general subjects of prophecy: (1) the audience of the prophets and (2) the prophets themselves. Because the books of Isaiah and Jeremiah are unusually long, this manual can treat only the large features and movements of the books. However, I have included some analytical studies, so that the reader can have the experience of personally analyzing the actual text. This, after all, is the major exercise of Bible study. The reader is urged to extend his analytical studies to other parts of the prophecies as well.

As you begin your study of Isaiah, Jeremiah, and Lamentations, prayerfully seek the help and instruction of the Holy Spirit, who knows the exact meaning of every word and sentence and whose ministry is to guide the believer into all truth (John 16:13). Hunger after God, and desire to know more about His ways. Your acquaintance with the prophets will help you in this quest, for, as Amos has written, "Truly the Lord God will not do anything unless He has revealed His secret to His servants the prophets" (3:7; *Berkeley*).

Lesson 1
The Audience
of the Prophets

Most messages of the Old Testament prophetic books were addressed to the generations of God's people who lived approximately between the years 840 and 420 B.C. The ten tribes, known specifically as the kingdom of Israel, lived in north Canaan (New Testament areas of Samaria and Galilee) before they were deported by the Assyrians in 722 B.C. The two tribes, known as the kingdom of Judah, lived in south Canaan before they were taken captive by the Babylonians in 586 B.C. This is shown on Chart A.

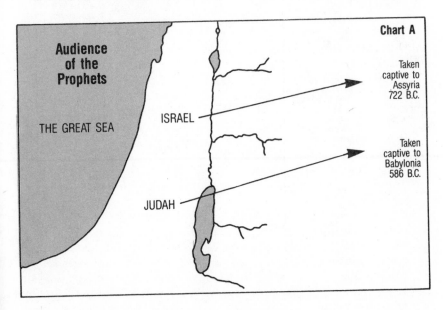

ISRAEL AND THE CHURCH IN THE BIBLE

Chart B

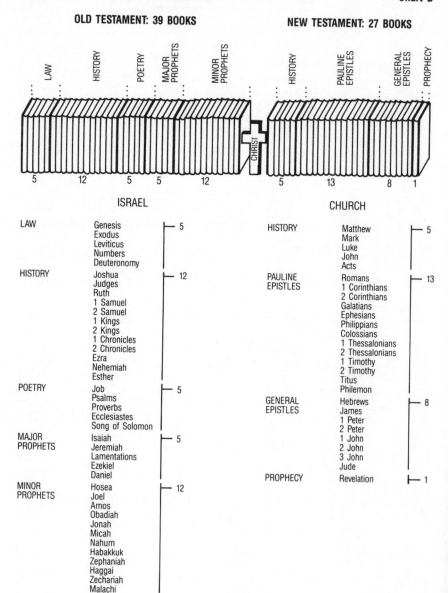

OLD TESTAMENT: 39 BOOKS

NEW TESTAMENT: 27 BOOKS

ISRAEL

LAW	Genesis Exodus Leviticus Numbers Deuteronomy	5
HISTORY	Joshua Judges Ruth 1 Samuel 2 Samuel 1 Kings 2 Kings 1 Chronicles 2 Chronicles Ezra Nehemiah Esther	12
POETRY	Job Psalms Proverbs Ecclesiastes Song of Solomon	5
MAJOR PROPHETS	Isaiah Jeremiah Lamentations Ezekiel Daniel	5
MINOR PROPHETS	Hosea Joel Amos Obadiah Jonah Micah Nahum Habakkuk Zephaniah Haggai Zechariah Malachi	12

CHURCH

HISTORY	Matthew Mark Luke John Acts	5
PAULINE EPISTLES	Romans 1 Corinthians 2 Corinthians Galatians Ephesians Philippians Colossians 1 Thessalonians 2 Thessalonians 1 Timothy 2 Timothy Titus Philemon	13
GENERAL EPISTLES	Hebrews James 1 Peter 2 Peter 1 John 2 John 3 John Jude	8
PROPHECY	Revelation	1

6

The people of God were not always divided into two camps. The split of the kingdom came at the end of Solomon's reign. Jeroboam I was the first king of the north, and Rehoboam the first king of the south. This story is recorded in 1 Kings 12–16.

The name Israel in the Old Testament sometimes refers to the entire nation; otherwise it refers to just the northern tribes. In this manual the name is used in the general sense unless otherwise stated. It is important for the student of the prophetic books to be acquainted with the audience of the prophets. In this lesson we shall learn about Israel's history and spiritual condition in the days of the prophets and also about the nation's place in God's sovereign plan.,

I. ISRAEL COMPARED WITH THE CHURCH

Broadly speaking, the great subject of the Old Testament is *Israel*, and the great subject of the New Testament is the *church*. Notice on Chart B how the structure of the Old Testament is built around *Israel*.

1. In the Pentateuch (books of Law) is recorded the *founding* of Israel.

2. In the twelve History books is recorded the *history* of Israel.

3. The five books of Poetry were written by spiritual leaders of Israel and contain *instructions* to Israel.

4. The seventeen books of Prophets contain *prophecies* concerning Israel.

The structure of the New Testament in the same way centers on the *church*.

1. In the gospels and the first two chapters of Acts is recorded the *founding* of the church.

2. The book of Acts narrates the *history* of the church for one generation.

3. The twenty-one Epistles were written by spiritual leaders of the church and contain *instructions* to the church.

4. The one book of Prophecy contains *prophecies* concerning the church.

There are many correspondences between Israel and the church concerning God's *purposes* in choosing them, *promises* given to them, and the *conditions* laid down for their blessing. Look at these on Chart C.

ISRAEL	CHURCH
PURPOSES	
1. **A Witness.** Witnessing unto the true God amid idolatrous nations of the world.	1. **A Witness.** Witnessing unto the Savior Jesus amid a lost world. (Read Acts 1:8.)
2. **A Demonstration.** Showing the blessedness of being God's people.	2. **A Demonstration.** Showing the blessedness of living in Christ.
3. **A Repository.** Preserving the revelations that God made to Israel of His character and His purposes.	3. **A Repository.** Preserving the marvelous truths of Christian doctrine that God has revealed to the church.
4. **A Channel.** Being a channel through which God's blessings might flow out to the surrounding Gentile nations.	4. **A Channel.** Being a channel today through which His blessings are reaching the whole world.
PROMISES	
1. **Purity.** Israel could be a pure nation spiritually and physically, by observing the Levitical laws of sacrifices and cleanliness. (Read Heb. 9:13.)	1. **Purity.** "How much more shall the blood of Christ . . . purge your conscience from dead works to serve the living God?" (Heb. 9:14).
2. **Wealth.** All other nations would borrow from Israel (Deut. 15:6).	2. **Wealth.** "Joint-heirs with Christ" (Rom. 8:17).
3. **Might.** No alliance of nations could conquer Israel (Ex. 33:2; Josh. 9:1-2).	3. **Might.** "Greater works than these shall he do; because I go unto my Father" (John 14:12).
4. **Reign.** Israel could be the ruling nation of the world, a theocracy, with God on the throne (Deut. 15:6).	4. **Reign.** Reigning with Christ in the Millennium (Rev. 20:6), and around the throne of God "for ever and ever" (Rev. 22:5).
CONDITIONS	
1. **Surrender.** The basic requirement for blessing was absolute and unconditional surrender to the will of God. This meant faith in God and obedience to His Word in all things (Deut. 26:16; Isa. 1:19).	1. **Surrender.** "If any man will come after me, let him deny himself, and take up his cross daily, and follow me" (Luke 9:23).
2. **Separation.** Israel was to be a separated people ("a peculiar people," Deut. 14:2), not intermarrying, intermingling, or indulging in the manners or customs of the idol-worshiping nations surrounding them (Ex. 33:16; Deut. 7:1-5).	2. **Separation.** "Ye are not of the world, but I have chosen you out of the world" (John 15:19). "And have no fellowship with the unfruitful works of darkness" (Eph. 5:11).
3. **Service.** The surrendered, separated Israelite was to **serve** his Lord. "And now, Israel, what doth the LORD thy God require of thee, but to fear the LORD thy God, to walk in all his ways, and to love him, and to serve the LORD thy God with all thy heart and with all thy soul" (Deut. 10:12).	3. **Service.** "Be ye stedfast, unmoveable, always abounding in the work of the Lord . . ." (1 Cor. 15:58). "With good will doing service, as to the Lord, and not to men" (Eph. 6:7).

II. ISRAEL'S HISTORY BRIEFLY SKETCHED

The history of Israel, as given in the Old Testament, generally falls into four periods, which may be remembered by four words, each beginning with the letter C: Camp, Commonwealth, Crown, Captivity. See Chart D.

ISRAEL'S HISTORY BY PERIODS   **Chart D**

IN EGYPT AND THE WILDERNESS	IN CANAAN UNDER JUDGES	IN CANAAN UNDER KINGS	IN ASSYRIA AND BABYLON
CAMP	COMMONWEALTH	CROWN	CAPTIVITY
660 YEARS	360 YEARS	460 YEARS	160 YEARS
PENTATEUCH	JOSHUA JUDGES RUTH	1 and 2 SAMUEL KINGS CHRONICLES	EZRA NEHEMIAH ESTHER

The *Camp Period* extended from the call of Abraham, the founder of the nation, to Moses' bringing the people up to the "gate" of Canaan, in the plains of Moab. This period lasted for about 660 years, the history of which is given in the Pentateuch.

The *Commonwealth Period* extended from Israel's entrance into Canaan under Joshua to the crowning of their first king, Saul. This period of about 360 years is described in Joshua, Judges, and Ruth.

The *Crown Period* extended from the crowning of their first king, Saul, to the Babylonian captivity. The period lasted about 460 years. Its history is recorded in the six books of Samuel, Kings, and Chronicles.

The *Captivity Period*, including the restoration, extended from the Babylonian captivity to the end of Old Testament history, a period of about 160 years. Its history is told in Ezra, Nehemiah, and Esther.

Let us look more closely at Israel's history during each of these four periods.

A. The Camp Period

This period is so called because during these years Israel was not permanently settled in any land as a nation. The people were first travelers from Ur to Canaan; then temporary dwellers in Canaan; then slaves in Egypt; and finally sojourners in the wildernesses of the Sinai Peninsula. Tents were their homes on all their journeys.

The Bible's record of this era of Israel's life is a fascinating one. We read how highly God favored this nation, visiting them in their bitterness and slavery in Egypt, and delivering them from their bondage. The story goes on to tell of His taking them into covenant relationship with Himself, choosing them from all other people to represent Him in the world, giving them laws that could not be surpassed, manifesting His presence among them, and giving them promises almost unbelievable in their scope and richness. God made possible for Israel, by fulfilling the two clear conditions of obedience and separation, to be the purest, richest, and most powerful people on the earth, and, as representatives of God, the rulers of the earth.

B. The Commonwealth Period

This new period began auspiciously. The nation, strong in faith, crossed the river Jordan under the leadership of Joshua. They conquered the enemy, drove most of them out of the land, and took possession of their inheritance. For a while they lived as God would have them live, true to Him and separated from all He had forbidden. For this God wonderfully blessed, protected, and empowered them. The greatest enemy cities, the strongest nations, and the most formidable alliances staggered before Israel when God was with them. And God was with Israel just as long as they were true to Him.

But soon the nation began its downward course. First, petty jealousies arose among the tribes. Next, there was distinct quarreling among themselves. Then there was a laxity in observing God's laws, and the people began to intermarry with idol worshipers. All through the Commonwealth Period there was growing discontent. Israel looked around on all the surrounding nations: Egypt to the southwest, Syria to the north, Assyria to the northeast, and Babylon to the east. They observed one thing that all these nations had in common: a human king sitting on a throne surrounded by courtiers and servants, with all the pomp and glitter and display that are so dear to the unregenerate human heart. Instead of glorying in that they were different from all these nations above which God had highly placed them, Israel began to despise their place of peculiarity and to be ashamed that they had no visible king as had these other nations.

Toward the end of Samuel's life this discontent broke out into open revolt, and the nation demanded a king. Chapter 8 of 1 Samuel tells the heartbreaking story (read this chapter now). The nation gave the plausible excuse for this step that Samuel was old and his sons wicked, but the real reason was that they despised their place of peculiarity and wanted to be "like all the nations," as is seen by verses 5, 19, and 20. God saw plainly that it was rejection of the Lord as King (v. 7). In verses 9 to 17 we have the description of a human king. Observe the emphasis on the personal pronouns in those verses, and you will see that the chief characteristic of those human kings was selfishness.

In spite of God's solemn warning of the consequences, the nation insisted upon having human kings. The kingdom was established, and for nearly five hundred years Israel struggled along under human kings, some good, some bad, some indifferent, but all immeasurably inferior to the divine King whom they had rejected. This is the story of the next period, the Crown Period.

C. The Crown Period

When Israel demanded a human king to replace their leader Samuel, they were really not rejecting Samuel, but the Lord. "The Lord said unto Samuel . . . they have not rejected thee, but they have rejected me, that I should not reign over them" (1 Sam. 8:7). One might wonder then, if they rejected the Lord, why the Lord would have any more to do with them. One reason is that although they rejected the Lord as their *King*, they still recognized Him as *God*. Their rejection of Him was not total. A stronger reason is that God, in His love and mercy, would offer them a new opportunity, in the new governmental setup, to recognize His authority by accepting *His* choice of kings and also by obeying those kings. (Read 1 Sam. 8:22; 9:16.)

The writing prophets, whose books we are studying in this Bible study series, ministered to Israel during much of the Crown Period, when the people were ruled by kings. It is important for us, therefore, to become acquainted with this era of human kings. A study of the books of Kings and Chronicles is good preparation for the study of the prophetical books.

The Crown Period covered about 460 years, extending from 1043 to 586 B.C. Look at Chart X and note the following:

1. *United kingdom*. Saul, David, and Solomon, the first three kings, each reigned over all twelve tribes of Israel. This constitut-

11

ed what is known as the United Kingdom. No writing prophets ministered at this time.

2. *Divided kingdom.* At the death of Solomon, his son Rehoboam took the throne. But Rehoboam acted in such a foolish, overbearing manner (1 Kings 12) that ten of the twelve tribes revolted and formed a new kingdom, choosing Jeroboam as their king and forming a new capital, Shechem in Samaria. For about two hundred years there were two kingdoms in Palestine, the ten tribes in the northern part of the country under the name of "Israel" and the two tribes still true to Solomon's son in the south, under the name of "Judah." This situation constituted what is known as the Divided Kingdom.

The kingdom of "Israel" was founded on idolatry (see 1 Kings 12:25-30) and went from bad to worse. All of Israel's nineteen kings were evil rulers. By 722 B.C. the ten tribes had grown so stubbornly idolatrous that God would bear with them no longer; He allowed the Assyrians to conquer them and take them out of their country as captives (see Chart A).

3. *Surviving kingdom.* After the ten tribes had been carried out of the land into captivity, the two tribes known as the kingdom of Judah remained in Canaan for almost 140 years. Judah had several good kings who brought the people back to a measure of obedience to God, but the poison of idolatry that had ended the northern kingdom destroyed Judah as well, and in 586 B.C. the two tribes were taken into Babylonian captivity, where they served seventy years (see Chart A).

D. The Captivity (and Restoration) Period

From the books of Esther, Daniel, and Ezekiel we get some idea of the life of the Jews in Babylon during their seventy-year captivity. Although the oppression cannot be said to have been severe, the hardships of physical, social, and religious deprivations were felt by all. Those of the believing remnant who determined to be true to their God especially felt the persecution of scorn and penalty.

In 539 B.C. Babylon fell to Cyrus, king of Persia, who favored the Jews by allowing them to return to Jerusalem to rebuild the Temple (Ezra 1:1-4). This was the first of two groups to return.

1. *First return.* Responding to Cyrus's permit, about 43,000 returned with Zerubbabel in 538 B.C. Work on the Temple was not begun until 536 B.C., seventy years after Nebuchadnezzar's siege of Jerusalem in 605 B.C.

2. *Second return.* In 458 B.C. another company of Jews, about 1,800, left Babylon for Jerusalem. This return was under the lead-

ership of Ezra, who was granted permission by Artaxerxes for the group to return. The purpose of Ezra's return was to carry out much needed religious reform among the Jews of the first return who had already drifted into apostasy.

Were the Jews of the two returns described above only from the kingdom of Judah? The answer to this question is furnished by the answer to another question: What eventually happened to the northern ten tribes, which had been taken captive by the Assyrians? T. Nicol writes,

> It must not be supposed that they became wholly absorbed in the population among whom they were settled. We can well believe that they preserved their Israelitish traditions and usages with sufficient clearness and tenacity, and that they became part of the Jewish dispersion so widespread throughout the East. It is quite possible that at length they blended with the exiles of Judah carried off by Nebuchadnezzar, and that then Judah and Ephraim became one nation as never before.[1]

Thus the captive Jews living around Babylon who were finally allowed to return to their homeland represented both the northern and southern kingdoms. In heart they were one people.

E. Israel's Crucial National Steps

Israel's history, from the time of the nation's calling to the present, is summarized in Chart E.
Note the following:

1. At the beginning of the Commonwealth Period, Israel was on a high pinnacle of opportunity. Jehovah was not only their God but He was their invisible King. His law regulated their conduct in every particular and in every walk of life. As long as Israel maintained this position of true worship and absolute obedience, nothing was impossible for them, for all the power of almighty God was theirs.

2. At the close of the Commonwealth Period the nation took a fearful downward step and rejected Jehovah as their King, demanding a human king to be their leader, counselor, and lawmaker. During the Crown Period, Jehovah appeared as their God but not as their King.

1. *The International Standard Bible Encyclopedia,* ed. James Orr (Grand Rapids: Eerdmans, 1952), 1: 571.

Chart E

ISRAEL'S CRUCIAL NATIONAL STEPS

God and King

① COMMONWEALTH
Invisible King

God — — —

② CROWN
Human kings

③ — — —
CAPTIVITY
No king

God — — —

④ RESTORATION

✝

God — — —

⑤ CONFRONTATION
King rejected

God — — —

⑥ DISPERSION
King sought

14

3. At the close of the Crown Period the nation took the second fearful downward step. They rejected Jehovah as their God, preferring the worship of idols made of wood and gold. So in the Captivity Period God did not appear in their *national* life or thought, either as God or King. There were individual Jews, however, who sought and worshiped God, and these composed a remnant of believers.

4. With permission from their captors, the believing remnant returned to their land, rebuilt the Temple, and began the worship of Jehovah as Lord, thus taking one big step upward.

5. When God appeared in the flesh, in the person of His Son, He offered Himself as their King, the Messiah, for whom they had been looking. This was Israel's great confrontation, the grand invitation to the kingdom of God, but the Jews rejected Jesus and crucified Him. ("His own received him not," John 1:11.)

6. Just as Israel was scattered among the nations for rejecting God as King during the Crown Period (Captivity), the Jews were dispersed throughout the world for rejecting Jesus as King (Dispersion). The Millennium will see the restoration of a remnant.

In this lesson we have surveyed the historical setting of the prophetical books. Our special interest has been the spiritual condition of God's people in the centuries just before and during the years when the prophets ministered. For these people were the *audience* of the prophets. Knowing something about the audience will help us to appreciate and understand the prophets' messages.

As a review for this lesson, write out the answers to the following questions:

1. What are some of the main differences between the Old and New Testaments?

_____

_____

_____

2. Compare Israel of the Old Testament and the church of the New Testament.

_____

_____

_____

3. Write out the fourfold purpose of God concerning Israel and the church.

_____

_____

_____

_____

_____

4. In your own words describe the four main periods of Israel's history in the Old Testament. Cite major events at the beginning and end of each period. Try to recall the significant dates.

_____

_____

_____

_____

_____

5. Name and describe the three divisions of the Crown Period.

_____

_____

_____

6. After Solomon's death, what caused ten of the tribes of Israel to revolt?

_____

7. How many kings of the northern kingdom were evil?

_____

Were any of Judah's kings good men?

_____

8. In which books of the Bible do we see the Jews as captives in Babylon?

_____

_____

9. What were some of the factors leading to the Jews' return to their land?

_____

Who was their leader in the first return?

_____

In the second return?

_____

10. Name and describe Israel's six crucial national steps.

_____

_____

_____

_____

Lesson 2
The Prophets of God

Prophet is an important word in the Bible, for it is one of the few official titles given to men of God who spoke His word to His people. In its various forms the word appears more than 660 times in the Bible, two-thirds of which are in the Old Testament.

In this lesson we will study the prophets in general, as introductory to the lessons devoted to Isaiah and Jeremiah, who were two of the Bible's prominent prophets of God.

I. THE PROPHETIC MINISTRY

The offices of judge, prophet, priest, and king were all important positions in Israel. Let us inquire into some of the distinctive functions of one of these—the prophet.

Our present inquiry is into some of the distinctive functions of the prophet.

A. The Term "Prophesy"

The primary task of the Old Testament prophets was not to *foretell future events but to forthtell* the will of God, which He had revealed to His prophets. Concerning the verb "prophesy," Gleason Archer writes:

> The Hebrew word is **nibba'** . . . a word whose etymology is much disputed. The best founded explanation, however, seems to relate this root to the Akkadian verb **nabu**, which means "to summon, announce, call. . . ." Thus the verb **nibba'**, one who has been called. On this interpretation the prophet was . . . one

called by God to proclaim as a herald from the court of heaven the message to be transmitted from God to man.[1]

B. Other Titles Applied to the Prophets

The prophets of the Old Testament were sometimes designated by other titles. Of these, three most frequently used were:
1. "man of God"—suggesting an intimate spiritual relationship
2. "seer"—suggesting perception of the true, and insight into the invisible things of God (cf. 1 Sam. 9:9)
3. "servant" of Jehovah
The prophets were also known as messengers of Jehovah, men of the Spirit (cf. Hosea 9:7), interpreters and spokesmen for God.

C. Qualifications of the Prophet

Listed below are some of the qualifications of the high office of the prophet. Considering the nature of the prophet's work, it does not surprise us that the qualifications were strict:
1. *Sovereign calling.* God's sovereign will determined who were His prophets (cf. Isa. 6; Jer. 1).
2. *Special abilities.* These were given by God's Spirit, enabling the prophet to perceive the truth (as "seer") and equipping him with the gift of communicating to people the revelation of God.
3. *Spiritual qualities.* These were not a few. Included were unselfishness, obedience to the voice of God, love and faith, courage and long-suffering.

D. Message of the Prophet

Whether the prophet was called to preach, or to write, or to do both, his message was the same. All the prophetic words of the Old Testament could probably be compiled under the following four large areas of truth about which the prophet engaged himself:
1. *Instruction of the great truths about God and man.* The prophets devoted much time telling the people about God—His character, His domain, His purposes, and His law. They also gave a true diagnosis of the spiritual health of the nation as a whole and of the individual souls.

---

1. Gleason L. Archer, *A Survey of Old Testament Introduction* (Chicago: Moody, 1964), p. 284.

2. *Warning and appeal to those living in sin.* It cannot be said that God brings judgment upon men without forewarning. Over and over again the prophets warned of judgment to come for sin and exhorted the people to repent and turn to God.

3. *Comfort and exhortation to those trusting and obeying God.* These are the warm and bright portions of the prophets' messages. The last part of Isaiah abounds in such notes of hope and consolation.

4. *Predictions of events to come.* Prophetic predictions were of two major subjects: (1) national and international events, of both the near and far-distant future; and (2) the comings of Jesus the Messiah—His first and second comings.

II. THE ORAL AND WRITING PROPHETS

All of God's prophets shared the same purpose for which they were divinely called. Their ministry primarily was to deliver to an unbelieving and apostate Israel a message from God (cf. Deut. 18:18-19). Some of these, now referred to as the writing (or literary) prophets, were chosen of God not only to a public-speaking ministry but also to be the authors of the inspired canonical books of prophecy. The others, now referred to as the oral prophets, ministered mostly by the spoken word.

A. The Oral Prophets

The Bible records the names of only a few of the oral prophets. And most of these names are not commonly known. Refer to Chart X and locate the following oral prophets: Ahijah, Iddo, Jehu, Elijah, Elisha, Oded, Shemaiah, Azariah, Hanani, Jahaziel, and Huldah. To this list might be added Nathan and Gad, of David's generation; Micaiah; and Eliezer. Which of these names do you recognize? You may want to look up any unfamiliar names in a Bible dictionary for a brief description of their part in Bible history. Note from Chart X that most of these prophets ministered before the appearance of the writing prophets.

The office of prophet probably originated around the time of Samuel, who founded and presided over various schools of young prophets ("company of the prophets," 1 Sam. 19:20). These prophets are also classified as oral prophets. Concerning these schools, *The Wycliffe Bible Commentary* states:

> The origin and history of these schools are obscure. According to [1 Sam.] 3:1, before the call of Samuel as a prophet, the prophetic word was rare in Israel, and prophecy was not wide-

20

spread. There is little doubt that these unions of prophets arose in the time of Samuel, and were called into existence by him. . . . These unions may have grown until the time of Elijah and Elisha. They arose only in Israel, not in Judah.[2]

B. The Writing Prophets

There are seventeen books of prophecy in our English Bible. These were written by sixteen different prophets, if Jeremiah wrote Lamentations as well as the book bearing his name. The books are classified as either Major or Minor, the classification assigned primarily for their relative length. As indicated in Lesson 1, these prophecies were written over a period of more than four centuries, from about 840 B.C. (Obadiah) to 420 B.C. (Malachi).

Writers of the Major Prophetical Books	Writers of the Minor Prophetical Books		
Isaiah	Hosea	Jonah	Zephaniah
Jeremiah	Joel	Micah	Haggai
Ezekiel	Amos	Nahum	Zechariah
Daniel	Obadiah	Habakkuk	Malachi

Chart F shows the three main periods during which the prophets ministered.

1. *Preexilic.* Eleven prophets ministered during the years leading up to the Assyrian captivity (722 B.C.). Notice the two big clusters of four prophets each:

TO ASSYRIAN CAPTIVITY: *Amos* and *Hosea*, prophets mainly to Israel; *Isaiah* and *Micah*, prophets mainly to Judah.
TO BABYLONIAN CAPTIVITY: *Nahum, Zephaniah, Jeremiah,* and *Habakkuk* (Judah)
THREE EARLIER PROPHETS: *Jonah* (Israel), *Obadiah,* and *Joel* (Judah)

2. *Exilic.* Two of the four major prophets were prophets of the Exile. They were *Ezekiel* and *Daniel.*

3. *Postexilic.* The three postexilic prophets were *Zechariah, Haggai,* and *Malachi.* The first two ministered in the early years of Israel's return to their land, whereas Malachi ministered at the close of this restoration period.

2. Charles F. Pfeiffer and Everett F. Harrison, eds., *The Wycliffe Bible Commentary* (Chicago: Moody, 1962), pp. 287-88.

21

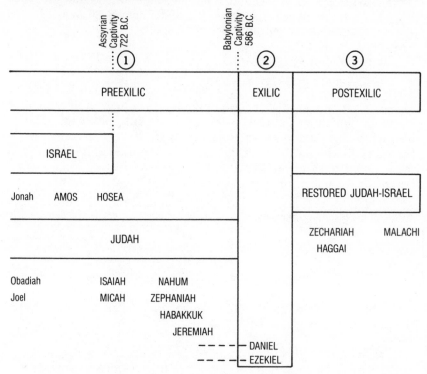

The writing prophets, in addition to composing their prophecies in written form, also had a wide ministry of speaking at public gatherings in the Temple or on the streets. For future generations of God's people, however, their major work was in their writing, and eternity will reveal fully how far-reaching that ministry was.

III. UNDERSTANDING THE PROPHETIC BOOKS

In order to derive the most profit from your study of the prophets, you should be acquainted with the following aspects of Bible history and prophecy:

A. History

In Lesson 1 of this manual you studied the important items of this historical background.

1. *Overall setting.* For each prophetic book there is both a large overall setting and the immediate setting. Concerning the

former, one must have some familiarity with the whole history of Israel in order to appreciate the utterances of the prophet, just as one would have to have some familiarity with the history of the United States to fully appreciate a Fourth of July oration, with its references to the flag, various battles, and so forth.

The large historical setting of the prophets was this: At the close of Samuel's judgeship, Israel had willfully insisted upon having human kings, in spite of God's solemn protest and warning of the consequences of such a step. God gave them what they demanded. These kings naturally had great power and influence. Many of them were wicked men and led multitudes into idolatry and all forms of disobedience to God. At such a time as this, God must speak. Although Israel had rejected God, God had not rejected Israel, and while their human kings were leading the people from Him, He, through the voice of the prophets, was seeking to woo them back to Himself. This was the occasion for the introduction of the prophets. The prophet was God's mouthpiece, speaking His warnings and predictions and exhortations.

2. *Immediate setting*. One must also understand something of the political and religious conditions that prevailed at the time any given prophet was speaking. For most of the prophetic books this can be ascertained by reading in the books of Kings and Chronicles the history of the kings who were ruling at any particular period. For example, the first verse of Isaiah gives the names of the four kings who were reigning while Isaiah was prophesying. By turning back to the historical books and reading the accounts of these reigns, one can realize the evils that existed and against which Isaiah was thundering.

The setting of foreign power also throws light on the prophetic books. For each book you will want to know something of the surrounding nations, especially those vying for world suzerainty. The three reigning world powers during the years of the prophets were:

Assyrian—up to 612 B.C. (fall of Nineveh)
Neo-Babylonian—up to 539 B.C. (fall of Babylon)
Persian—up to Malachi (and beyond)

3. *Philosophy of history*. You will appreciate and understand more of the historical movements of the prophets' days if you always keep in mind that human history is in the sovereign hands of an omniscient, omnipotent God. Everything transpires either by His permissive or directive will. He foreknows every event before it becomes history, and on many occasions He gave such prophetic revelation to His prophets to share with the nations.

4. *The chosen nation*. Israel was God's elect nation, called into being by His sovereign decree and preserved through the

ages (sometimes in a very small remnant) in fulfillment of His covenant originally made with Abraham.

B. Prophecy

1. *The prophets' twofold ministry.* Remember that the prophets had a twofold mission: one for the immediate present, their own time; and one for the future, predicting events. The primary object that the prophets had in view was to testify against, and to arrest the sins of, their own time. Their second object was to foretell the future as God revealed it to them.

2. *The four prophetic points.* The utterances of the prophets for the most part centered on four points in history: (1) their own time; (2) the threatening captivities (Assyrian and Babylonian) and subsequent restoration; (3) the coming of their Messiah; and (4) the Millennium. This is illustrated by Chart G.

It was as though the prophet were on some high eminence (see "A" on Chart G) looking off into the distance and speaking of what he saw. Most often he saw the sins that prevailed in his own day and spoke of them (see "1" on Chart G.). Then he would look off to the day when the nation would be taken out of its land into captivity. He also saw an eventual regathering of the Jews from the captivities (see "2" on Chart G). At times the Spirit enabled him to look further into the future and foretell of the coming Messiah

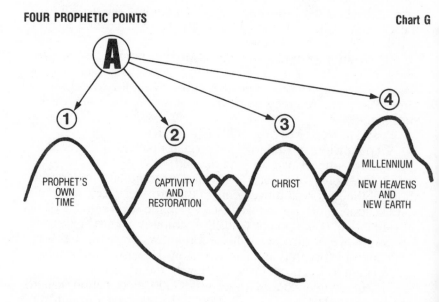

FOUR PROPHETIC POINTS **Chart G**

PROPHET'S OWN TIME

CAPTIVITY AND RESTORATION

CHRIST

MILLENNIUM NEW HEAVENS AND NEW EARTH

(see "3" on Chart G). Occasionally he saw still further and spoke of a glorious time of restoration and peace coming to God's people in the Millennium (see "4" on Chart G).

In order to get the true meaning of the words of a prophet, one must determine in each individual utterance which of these four events is his subject.[3] The very language of the prophet and the context in which he speaks the words usually indicate this. For example, read Isaiah 53 and determine to which of these four points in history (as indicated on Chart G) the prophet is referring.

3. *The two messianic themes.* When a prophet speaks of Christ, he refers to Him either in the first coming, as the suffering Messiah (e.g., Isa. 53), or in the second coming, as the reigning Messiah (e.g., Isa. 11). The prophets were not aware that a long interval would transpire between Christ's manifestation in suffering (first advent) and Christ's revelation in glory (second advent). His suffering and His reigning appeared to them to be very close in time. The student of prophecy must keep this in mind when he studies the predictive sections of the prophetic books.

In this lesson you have been studying about the prophets of God in general. Keep all these things in mind as you move on to the next lessons and study about two of the major prophets, Isaiah and Jeremiah. The questions given below will help you review the major sections of this lesson.

1. Describe the ministry to which the prophets were called.

_____

_____

2. Name three qualifications for the office of prophet.

_____

_____

_____

_____

3. Sometimes a prophecy may have a multiple intention of fulfillment (e.g., a prophecy of restoration of the Jews may concern [1] return from Babylonian captivity and [2] regathering of Israel from all parts of the world in the end times).

25

3. Identify four main points of the prophet's message.

_____

_____

_____

_____

_____

4. Name the writing prophets and some of the oral prophets.

_____

_____

_____

_____

5. What were the three periods during which the writing prophets ministered?

_____

_____

_____

_____

Locate each prophet according to period.

_____

_____

_____

_____

6. What were the four points in history on which the utterances of the prophets, for the most part, centered?

_____

_____

_____

_____

Lesson 3
The Man Isaiah

While studying a book written by a prophet, it is helpful to have a mental image of the book's author. His family background, his character, and his personal history are some of the things that form such an image. So the object of this lesson is to study the man Isaiah.

I. HIS NAME

The name Isaiah translates a short form of the prophet's Hebrew name, *Yeshaiah*. The long form, which is how his name appears in his book and all other Old Testament references, is *Yeshayahu*. This is a compound name having such meanings as "Jehovah saves," "Jehovah is salvation," and "salvation of Jehovah."

Surely the prophet was given this name by divine design. Whenever people mentioned his name, they were audibly reiterating the great theme of his message. In the book that he wrote, two of his favorite words are those translated "he shall save" and "salvation."

II. HIS RANK AMONG THE PROPHETS

Of all the writing prophets, Isaiah is justly accounted the greatest. His prophecy is one of the longest, is quoted in the New Testament more frequently than any other, and he more often than any other prophet tells of the coming Messiah. Isaiah prophesied for about fifty years (see Chart H) during critical times of both kingdoms, Israel and Judah. He was greatly responsible for the sweeping reforms introduced by Hezekiah, who was one of Judah's righteous kings.

Merrill Unger says this of Isaiah:

Isaiah . . . is the great messianic prophet and prince of OT seers. For splendor of diction, brilliance of imagery, versatility and beauty of style, profundity and breadth of prophetic vision, he is without peer.[1]

Read some of the New Testament passages where Isaiah is quoted or referred to. Some are listed below. (Note: In the King James Version his name is Esaias, after the Greek spelling of the name.)

Cited by	Passages	Isaiah Passages Quoted
Matthew	Matthew 4:14-16; 8:17; 12:17-21	9:1-2; 53:4; 42:1-4
John the Baptist	John 1:23	40:3
Jesus	Luke 4:16-21	61:1-2
Apostle John	John 12:38-41	53:1; 6:9-10
Ethiopian treasurer	Acts 8:28	53:7-8
Paul	Acts 28:25-27;	6:9-10; 10:22-23; 11:5; 1:9;
	Romans 9:27, 29; 10:16, 20; 15:12	53:1; 65:1; 11:10

III. TIMES IN WHICH HE LIVED

The dates of Isaiah's birth and death are unknown. If the date of Isaiah 7:3 is around 734 B.C., and if Isaiah's son at that time was not a mere child, Isaiah may have been born about 760 B.C. "His early years were therefore spent in the prosperous, luxurious and careless days of king Uzziah, the conditions of which are reflected in chapters ii., ii."[2]

From Isaiah 1:1 we learn that most of his public ministry took place during the reigns of these kings of Judah: Uzziah, Jotham, Ahaz, and Hezekiah. It is possible that he did no public preaching after Manasseh succeeded Hezekiah on the throne. Consult a Bible dictionary for a review of the careers of each of the above-named kings.

Study carefully Chart H, and compare it with the larger Chart X.

Observe from the chart that Hosea and Micah were contemporary prophets with Isaiah (cf. Hos. 1:1 and Mic. 1:1). Isaiah prophesied during the last seventeen years of the northern kingdom. His message, however, was primarily to the southern kingdom. When Israel's throne was tottering because of sin, Judah also was following her sister kingdom in the downward path, though with slower steps.

1. Merrill F. Unger, *Unger's Bible Handbook* (Chicago: Moody, 1966), p. 306.
2. G.T. Manley, ed., *The New Bible Handbook* (Chicago: InterVarsity, 1950), p. 214.

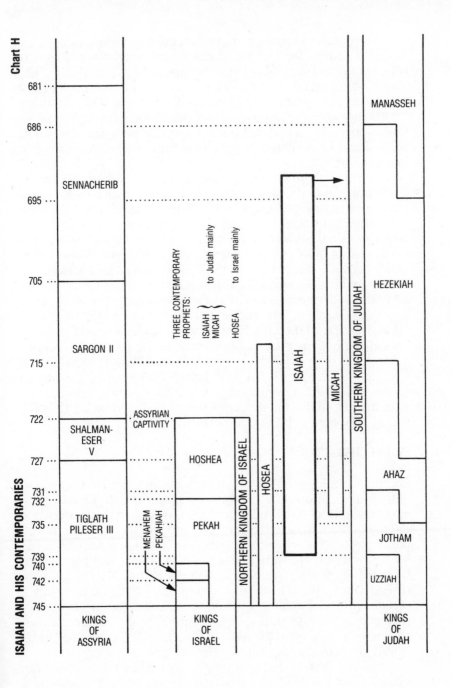

Chart H

ISAIAH AND HIS CONTEMPORARIES

THREE CONTEMPORARY
PROPHETS:
ISAIAH ⎫
MICAH ⎭ to Judah mainly
HOSEA   to Israel mainly

| KINGS OF ASSYRIA | | KINGS OF ISRAEL | NORTHERN KINGDOM OF ISRAEL | HOSEA | ISAIAH | MICAH | SOUTHERN KINGDOM OF JUDAH | KINGS OF JUDAH |

681
686
695
705
715
722
727
731
732
735
739
740
742
745

SENNACHERIB

SARGON II

SHALMAN-
ESER
V

TIGLATH
PILESER III

ASSYRIAN
CAPTIVITY

MENAHEM
PEKAHIAH

HOSHEA

PEKAH

MANASSEH

HEZEKIAH

AHAZ

JOTHAM

UZZIAH

29

To refresh the memory regarding the historical setting of Isaiah, read 2 Kings 14–21. King Uzziah's early reign was a successful one, but toward the end of his life he strayed far from God (read 2 Chron. 26:16-23). His son Jotham, who succeeded him, "did that which was right in the sight of the Lord" (2 Chron. 27:2). Although he was not able to lead the people out of their corrupt ways, Jotham apparently supported Isaiah's spiritual program. But when, at his death, his son Ahaz mounted the throne, affairs took a different turn.

During Jotham's reign, clouds had begun to gather on the political horizon in the shape of a military combination of Syria and Israel against Judah (2 Kings 15:37). When Ahaz became king of Judah, instead of searching out and dealing with the national sins for which God was allowing this chastisement, he formed an alliance with the king of Assyria, an alliance that in the days of his son Hezekiah proved almost fatal to the kingdom. He also introduced idolatry, with all its attendant evils, and even caused God's holy altar to be set to one side and one of heathen design put in its place.

King Hezekiah, who succeeded Ahaz, honored Jehovah in his administration of the kingdom. But such leadership and example brought only a measure of obedience on the part of the people. Though the outward form and ceremony of Temple worship was kept up, all manner of sins were being committed by the people —sins of idolatry, covetousness, impurity, injustice, and oppression. Against all this the prophet's voice needed to be lifted. Isaiah was just the man to be God's spokesman at such a time.

IV. HIS CHARACTER

Isaiah was bold, fearless, and absolutely sincere. He seemed to glory in the opportunity to talk to his fellow countrymen in plain language and to show them how they looked in God's sight. He did not hesitate to face a wicked king and tell him the most unwelcome truths. This prince of prophets lived not for court favor but for divine favor. He went before a sinful people and plainly told them that they were insulting God and tempting Him to the limit of endurance. He warned that, unless they changed their ways, certain and awful judgment would come to the nation. No class of society escaped his scathing denunciations. Kings, officers, priests, common people, even the women (Isa. 3:16-26), were unsparingly told just how they appeared in God's sight.

Isaiah was stern and uncompromising when the occasion demanded, but he also had a tender heart. He warned of judgment because he loved his people, and like a loving mother he tenderly wooed them to heed his counsel so that they could claim the prospects of a glorious future. This is exactly what one would expect of Isaiah when it is remembered that a prophet was but the mouthpiece of God, reflecting His feelings toward sin and also toward His beloved people.

Isaiah was also a man of great spirituality and strong faith. Associating so intimately and constantly with God, he had no place for worldliness and doubt. He saw men and things from God's point of view, in the light of eternity.

Isaiah was a many-sided genius. His ministry of prophecy was enhanced by his being gifted as a poet, a statesman, and an orator.

V. HIS PERSONAL HISTORY

Little is known of Isaiah's personal history. Emphasis in the Bible is on the message rather than on the man. All we know of his parentage is that he was the son of Amoz (Isa. 1:1; not the prophet Amos). His father may have been a person of prominence, for thirteen times in the Old Testament Isaiah is referred to as the "son of Amoz."

A Jewish tradition says that Isaiah was of royal descent, a brother of King Amaziah and so a cousin of King Uzziah. His writings show that he was blessed with a fine intellect and a good education. He was perfectly familiar with the Scriptures and well posted on the political affairs of his day.

Isaiah was married, and his wife was a prophetess (Isa. 8:3). He had two sons whose names were Maher-shalal-hash-baz ("he hasteneth to prey," 8:3) and Shear-jashub ("a remnant shall return," 7:3). These peculiar names illustrated the two great points in Isaiah's message to the nation. First, if the nation refused to turn from their idolatry and sin, God would punish them by allowing a nation to conquer them and carry them out of their land to remain captive in another country for many years. The picture is that of a ferocious wolf pouncing upon a lamb and taking it away to his den. The second name symbolically prophesied that after God had punished the nation by this captivity He would allow His people to return to their own land but that only a remnant would avail themselves of this opportunity.

The time and circumstances of Isaiah's death are not known. According to tradition (Talmud) he was sawn asunder by the wicked King Manasseh (cf. 2 Kings 21:16; Heb. 11:37).

VI. HIS CALL

Isaiah must have received his call to the prophetic office at an early age. He describes the circumstances vividly in chapter 6. We shall study this in detail in a later lesson, but it would be profitable to read the chapter now to understand more fully what impelled Isaiah to be the prophet that he was.

How this vision of God's greatness, holiness, and glory changed Isaiah's life! Recall the similar experiences of Moses (Ex. 3) and Saul of Tarsus (Acts 9). When God showed Himself in a vision to these men, they recognized themselves as vile, worthless creatures, with no power or wisdom of their own. They surrendered to God and wholly committed themselves to do His bidding, whatever it might be. Isaiah's words of consecration have been an inspiration and challenge to multitudes of God's servants: "Here am I; send me" (6:8).

VII. HIS MESSAGE

Isaiah, like most of the prophets, preached a twofold message: warning of judgment for sin, and comfort of salvation for righteousness. In his book the two themes stand out in bright contrast. John Phillips writes, "One moment his book is black with the thunder and the darkness of the storm. The next, the rainbow shines through, and he sweeps his readers on to the Golden Age that still lies ahead for the world."[3] Isaiah spoke mainly to the chosen people of God, but his message was also directed to foreign nations, prophesying judgment but proclaiming the evangel to them as well. (Read 11:10; 42:6; 45:22.)

Isaiah is known mostly for his messianic prophecies. Some of these, such as chapter 53, are classic examples of literature at its finest. There are more messianic prophecies in Isaiah than in any other prophetic book. Unger says, "Every glory of our Lord and every aspect of His life on the earth are set forth in this great evangelical prophecy."[4] As a short exercise read the following passages and note what each prophecy of Christ contributes to the topics listed:

Salvation: 12:1-2; 40:10; 52:7; 61:1

_____

_____

Pardon: 6:7; 40:2; 53:5; 55:7

_____

_____

3. John Phillips, *Exploring the Scriptures* (Chicago: Moody, 1965), p. 131.
4. Unger, ibid. p. 307.

Cleansing: 1:18, 25; 27:9; 52:15

_____

_____

Peace: 9:6; 26:12; 32:17; 53:5

_____

_____

Continue this exercise by reading the following passages. List
what each says about Christ:
7:14-15

_____

8:8

_____

9:1-2, 7

_____

11:1-2

_____

35:5-6

_____

40:12-18

_____

42:1-3

_____

50:5-6

_____

51:13

_____

52:13-14

_____

53:1-12

_____

59:20

_____

61:2

_____

One can readily see why Isaiah is called the evangelical prophet. He speaks of Christ and of His redemption with almost the same clearness and fullness as any of the New Testament writers. The way of salvation is plainly and simply set forth. In the book of Isaiah, Christ's portrait is painted by the divine Artist with such accuracy that all the essential features of His person and work are brought before us. In the passage you have just studied you have seen prophecies concerning such things as His virgin birth, human and divine names, twofold nature, humiliation, sacrifice, and exaltation.

1. What kings of Judah were reigning during Isaiah's public ministry?

2. State briefly the character of each of these kings.

3. What was the political condition of the nation during Isaiah's lifetime?

What was the religious condition?

4. What other prophets ministered about the same time as Isaiah?

To what kingdoms did they speak?

5. Describe briefly Isaiah's character.

_____

_____

_____

_____

6. What is known about his family?

_____

_____

7. What were the symbolic meanings of the names of Isaiah's sons?

_____

_____

8. Describe Isaiah's vision and call.

_____

_____

_____

_____

9. What were the main themes of Isaiah's message?

_____

_____

_____

10. Compare Isaiah with the other Old Testament prophets.

_____

_____

_____

Lesson 4
The Book of Isaiah

Let us look at the book of Isaiah as a whole, in order to appreciate its major contributions to the Scriptures. We shall first observe some of the main characteristics of Isaiah's writing and then study the book's structure, main contents, and applications.

I. THE STYLE OF ISAIAH'S WRITINGS

The book of Isaiah is basically a series of discourses by the prophet delivered at different times and on different occasions. The arrangement of these discourses is generally chronological whenever history is involved.[1] The topical arrangement will be studied later in this lesson when a survey is made of the book.

Isaiah's style is lofty and strongly rhetorical. He excelled as an orator and designed his discourses to attract and stir his audiences. Though his writing is not poetry, he uses many of the devices of the poet, especially figures of speech. He excels in variety of vocabulary and in the use of words to convey powerful truths.

A. Figures of Speech

Isaiah's figurative language is a distinctive feature of his style of writing. The figures he uses are varied and expressive, and as a master orator he changes with lightning rapidity from one figure of speech to another. Only a few of these are cited here.

Personification is found throughout the book. Observe the lofty, oratorical figure with which Isaiah begins his first address, 1:2. The picture is of a court of justice, with the Lord as Judge calling upon the heavens and the earth to sit as a jury and listen to His

---

1. The datelines (specific references to dates) of Isaiah are 1:1; 6:1; 7:1; 14:28; 20:1; 36:1.

indictment against His people. At verse 5 God seems to turn from the jury and address His words to the nation (see vv. 5-20). Note how the tone changes at verse 18. God abruptly turns from accusation and threats to reason and pleading with the people (vv. 18-20).

In 1:5-6 the nation is spoken of as a beaten victim whose sores have not been treated. Verse 7 explains what the blows were that had fallen upon the nation in God's endeavor to turn her from sin. At verse 21 the figure is changed, and God speaks of the nation as an unfaithful wife. In chapter 5 the nation is referred to as a vineyard, in another place as a besieged city, and so on.

A striking figure occurs in chapter 8. The nation is represented as refusing "the waters of Shiloah" (the things and the ways of God), preferring those of pagans. God assures them that they shall have enough, and more than enough, of heathen ways. Assyria under the figure of a river is described as rushing in and overflowing the land. The flood rises higher and higher, even to the neck, leaving nothing but the head above water, until, nearly drowned by the fearful deluge, the nation cries out, "O Immanuel." Read 8:5-8 with this thought in mind and observe Isaiah's poetical way of wording this prophecy. The prophecy itself was fulfilled in the reign of Hezekiah when the Assyrians did come up and fill the land and destroy the cities. They even threatened the head, Jerusalem, when Hezekiah's cry to God brought deliverance. (Read 2 Chron. 32:1-23.)

Notice once more an instance of this poetic and figurative way in which Isaiah predicts coming events. The plain fact that he wishes to predict in chapter 5 is that God, who controls all nations, is going to punish Judah by summoning the other nations and allowing them to conquer her and to carry her away captive. But observe the language he employs to prophesy this. (Read 5:26-29; 7:18-20.)

Similes and metaphors also appear frequently in Isaiah. (Simile: the comparison of things with the use of "like" or "as"; metaphor: an implied comparison, without those words.) At times Isaiah uses paranomasia (play on words) and alliteration (repetition of the same first letter or sound of words or lines), which are usually not evident in the English translation.

B. Satire

Satire is the use of sarcasm or irony to expose or rebuke actions and attitudes. Isaiah's sarcasm should not be overlooked when considering the style of his writing. His one grand object was to turn the people from sin, especially the sin of idolatry. He used various means at his command to accomplish this purpose. Sometimes he sought to frighten them into obedience to God by scathing denunciations and dreadful threats. At other times he tried to woo them from their perilous course by tender appeal. Perhaps the most biting and stinging method he employed was that of satire. For example he tried to make the people realize how utterly absurd and foolish idolatry was, to say nothing of its being sinful.

Read the following passages, which are examples of Isaiah's use of satire. What is Isaiah's point in each case?

40:19-20

_____

41:6-7

_____

44:13-20 (this is a classic example of the folly of idolatry)

_____

C. Similarity of Outline

In character and broad outline many of Isaiah's discourses are similar. The following four points can usually be seen in such discourses: (1) indictment or accusation; (2) threat; (3) exhortation or entreaty; (4) promise of purification or blessing.

The first discourse, chapter 1, is an illustration of this.
1. The Indictment or Accusation (vv. 1-9)
2. The Threat (vv. 10-15)
3. The Exhortation or Entreaty (vv. 16-20)
4. The Promise of Purification and Blessing (vv. 21-31)

D. Songs in Isaiah

Although Isaiah is not a book of poetry, various songs and refrains appear throughout the book. Some of the more prominent ones are:
1. Song of the Vineyard (chap. 5)
2. Song of the Redeemed (chap. 12)
3. Song of the Blossoming Desert (chap. 35)
4. Song of the Restored Wife (chap. 54)

II. THE STRUCTURE OF ISAIAH

Most of your study thus far has been *about* Isaiah—the man and the book. The time has arrived for you to begin a methodical study of *the text itself*. The order of study is, first, survey of the

SURVEY CHART OF ISAIAH
ISAIAH THE GLORIOUS THRONE OF JEHOVAH THE HOLY ONE

Chart I

A key verse: 6:3

		JUDGMENT OF GOD		COMFORT OF GOD	

| | Uzziah Jotham Ahaz | | | Hezekiah | True God | Suffering Messiah | Reigning Lord |

| JUDAH PROPHECIES | FOREIGN PROPHECIES | WARNINGS AND PROMISES | HISTORICAL SECTION | REDEMPTION PROMISED | REDEMPTION PROVIDED | REDEMPTION REALIZED |

13   28   36   40   49   58   66

holiness, righteousness, and justice of God

grace, compassion, and glory of God

GOD'S GOVERNMENT

GOD'S GRACE

"a throne" (6:6)

"Lamb . . . in the midst of the throne" (Rev. 7:17)

"a lamb" (53:7)

HOLY →   ← GLORY

39

whole; then analysis of the parts. This is the time for the survey study.

Follow the procedures of survey study outlined in other manuals of this self-study series. For such a survey study you should scan the entire book of Isaiah, observing and recording the following:

1. chapter titles (record these on a survey chart similar to chart I)

2. key words and phrases

3. your main impressions

As you continue your survey study, you will want to locate groupings of subject matter leading to various outlines. Eventually determine a theme, title, and key verse.

Refer to Chart I as an aid to your own survey study.

Broadly speaking, there are two main parts in the book of Isaiah, the division coming between chapters 39 and 40. There are identified on Chart I as (1) Judgment of God and (2) Comfort of God.

A. Judgment

Judgment is the prominent thought of the first division of Isaiah —judgment on Judah and Jerusalem for their sins, and judgment on the nations that are hostile to the chosen people. But although judgment is the keynote of this first division, scattered here and there are promises for Judah and hopes for both Jew and Gentile in the predictions of the Messiah. Amid the darkness there are frequent flashes of the "great light" mentioned in chapter 9:2; glimpses of the "bright and morning star" (see Rev. 22:16) and the coming Redeemer, of whom Isaiah speaks so fully in the later chapters.

Looking more closely at the chapters, it is convenient for study to subdivide this first division. For example, the chart shows that the first twelve chapters are discourses addressed chiefly to Judah and Jerusalem; chapters 13–27 are discourses regarding the nations that were hostile to Judah; chapters 28–35, various warnings and promises; and the last four chapters of the section are purely historical, being a review of Hezekiah's reign, given in 2 Kings 18–20. Recall from Chart H when Hezekiah reigned as king.

B. Comfort

In the second division of the book (chaps. 40–66), *comfort* is the predominant note, although there are repeated warnings to the wicked.

The discourses in this division are chiefly predictive. They fall into three groups of nine chapters each. Read 48:22 and 57:21 and observe the common utterance, "No peace, saith my God, to the wicked," which concludes each of the first two groups.

The first of the three groups (chaps. 40–48) compares Jehovah, the true God, with idols, the false gods. The second group (chaps. 49–57) speaks almost entirely concerning the Messiah. The third group (chaps. 58–66) describes the final restoration of God's people, with God on the throne (66:1) acknowledged as Lord over all (66:23).

Note also the following outline on the chart:

Redemption Promised
Redemption Provided
Redemption Realized

In your survey reading of Isaiah observe how the above outlines represent the various sections. Study the other parts of Chart I for what they contribute to an understanding of the overall message of Isaiah.

An easy way to remember the broad organization of Isaiah by chapters is:

1. Isaiah has sixty-six chapters. The Bible has sixty-six books.

2. Isaiah has two main divisions: the first, of thirty-nine chapters; and the second, of twenty-seven chapters. The Bible has two main parts: the Old Testament, of thirty-nine books; and the New Testament, of twenty-seven books.

3. The prevailing note in the first division of Isaiah is *judgment*; in the second division, *comfort*. The prevailing note of the Old Testament is *law*; of the New Testament, *grace*.

4. In the first section of Isaiah, there are frequent allusions to and predictions of the Messiah; but He is described with great fullness in the second. In the Old Testament there are frequent allusions to Christ in types and prophecies; but in the New Testament He is presented in all His fullness.

III. ISAIAH'S PROPHETIC PERSPECTIVE

Isaiah, like many of the prophets, was given divine revelation concerning four prophetic points: (1) the prophet's own time, (2) coming captivity, (3) coming of Christ, and (4) new heavens and new earth. (See Chart G.) How these are distributed throughout the book is summarized as follows:

1. *The prophet's own time.* Messages concerning this appear throughout the book. Forthtelling was Isaiah's major role.

2. *Captivity.* Isaiah foresaw Judah taken captive by the Babylonians. God alone knew when the captivity would come (586 B.C.).

41

The first mention of Babylon (Shinar) as the captor is in 11:11. In the days of King Hezekiah the prophecy was made clear (cf. 39:6).

3. *Coming of Christ.* These prophecies abound in the Book of Consolation (chaps. 40–66). They concern both the first and second comings of Christ.

4. *New heavens and new earth.* Isaiah prophesies of end times, especially with reference to the Millennium, with Christ as the Prince of peace (9:6) and the elect nation of Israel gathered together after its worldwide dispersion (27:12-13; 43:5-7; 65:8-10). On the most distant horizon he sees the new heavens and a new earth (65:17).

IV. A SUMMARY OF THE CONTENTS OF ISAIAH

Isaiah is a book about "the Glorious Throne of Jehovah, the Holy One."[2] An appropriate key verse is "Holy, holy, holy, is the Lord of hosts: the whole earth is full of his glory" (6:3). The two themes that are developed under this title, as indicated by the two grand divisions of the survey chart, are judgment (chaps. 1–39) and comfort (chaps. 40–66).

V. ISAIAH'S MESSAGE FOR TODAY

The Holy Spirit inspired Isaiah to record a divine message not only for his day but for ours. How does his message apply today? As a concluding exercise for this lesson, list the prominent truths taught by Isaiah that are applicable today. List a few for each category shown:

The nature of God

_____

_____

The government of God

_____

_____

The salvation of God

_____

_____

2. The phrase "Holy One of Israel" is Isaiah's favorite reference to God. It appears more than twenty-five times in the book (first appearance: 1:4).

The saved people: Jews

_____

Gentiles

_____

The future of Israel

_____

The comings of the Messiah

_____

2. Describe the style of Isaiah's writing.

_____

_____

_____

3. In your own words, what is the main theme of Isaiah?

_____

What are the two supporting themes?

_____

4. Describe the main content of each of the three sections of chapters 40–66.

_____

_____

_____

Isaiah's Vision of Judah

The message Isaiah preached to Judah and Jerusalem was the one he received by revelation from God. God gave Isaiah Spirit-inspired perception to see things *as God saw them* and to react and speak as God wanted to use him.

This lesson is devoted to an analysis of chapter 1. In this opening chapter of Isaiah's book we have an example of the kind of message Isaiah delivered to his people. It is an appropriate introduction to the entire book. The next two lessons are devoted to two important passages in Isaiah—6:1-13, which records Isaiah's divine call; and 52:13–53:12, which is one of the Bible's prominent messianic prophecies.

I. ANALYSIS OF 1:1-31

First mark off this chapter in your Bible into these three parts: verses 1-9; verses 10-20; verses 21-31. Then read through the chapter, keeping these segment divisions in mind. Mark your Bible as you read, underlining key words, phrases, and verses. What are your first impressions of this chapter?

Note the phrase "The vision...which he saw" in the title verse (1:1). Can one fully understand the process of divine inspiration? How does such a God-man situation point to the process as being a miracle?

Analyze each of the three segments individually at first. Comparisons may be made later. Using Chart J as a pattern for recording your observations on paper, proceed with your analysis.

A. 1:2-9

1. Use the paragraph divisions shown. Record your own paragraph title in the upper right-hand corner of each paragraph box.

1:2-9 UNFAITHFULNESS	1:10-20 HYPOCRISY	1:21-31 WORLDLINESS

	2a The Lord hath spoken	10 Hear the word of the Lord	21 Harlot
The Sin	2b	11	Apostasy
		Vain Oblations	
	5		24 Restore
The Conse-quences	7	16	Restoration I will restore
		Solutions Come . . . let us	28 Consumed
Remnant Spared	9 Except the Lord . . . had	Options	Judgment
		19	
		20	31

How does verse 2*a* introduce the segment?

_____

_____

Who is the speaker?

_____

_____

Who is the audience?

_____

_____

45

What is significant about such an audience?

_____

_____

2. What is the main point of each paragraph?

_____

_____

_____

_____

Make a simple outline of this segment. Compare yours with the one shown.
3. Note the various synonyms for "sin" in verses 2-4, and the various kinds of sin exposed. List these.

_____

_____

_____

_____

4. God is referred to as the "Holy One of Israel" in verse 4. This was Isaiah's favorite title for God, probably coined by him. What does the title connote?

_____

_____

(Note: The name "Israel" is used here and in similar contexts to denote all the covenant people of God, not the northern kingdom exclusively.)
5. Compare the figurative language of verses 5-6 and the literal language of verses 7-8. What is each pair of verses describing?

_____

_____

_____

As of the time of writing, was the judgment past, future, or both?

_____

_____

(See Comments.)

6. Who speaks the words of verse 9?

_____

Recall the story of Sodom and Gomorrah, referred to here. Read Romans 9:22-29 to see how Paul uses this verse in his exposition. What great truth is in the word "Except the Lord . . . had" (v. 9)?

_____

_____

B. 1:10-20

1. Follow the paragraph divisions shown. Compare the atmosphere of verses 11-15 with that of verses 16-18.

_____

_____

_____

2. Why did Isaiah mention Sodom and Gomorrah in the introductory verse 10?

_____

3. What is the indictment of verses 11-15?

_____

_____

Account for God's severe reaction to the sins described.

_____

4. What is the solution of the problem just described, according to verses 16-18?

_____

Observe the many commands. Do these verses suggest salvation by works? Who gives the cleansing, and who makes the transformation referred to in verse 18?

_____

_____

_____

5. What are the options and conditions cited by the last paragraph?

_____

_____

_____

_____

C. 1:21-31

1. What is the main point of each paragraph?

_____

_____

Observe the word "become" in the first paragraph. What brings on such changes in the heart of a man?

_____

_____

2. Observe how God takes the initiative in the restoration described in the middle paragraph. Relate the words "righteousness" and "faithful" of verse 26 to the same words in verse 21.

_____

_____

_____

3. Upon whom is the judgment of verses 28-31?

_____

_____

Why would these not come under the redemptive work of verses 24-27?

_____

_____

_____

Consider verses 19-20 for your answer to this question.
4. As you compare these three segments, note the major sin exposed in each; the message of salvation in each; and references to

judgment in each. How adequately does this chapter reveal the message that Isaiah was to preach?

_____

_____

5. What are the various names and titles of God in this chapter?

_____

_____

Study the context of each. What attributes are ascribed to God?

_____

_____

6. List some important spiritual applications that may be derived from this chapter.

_____

_____

_____

_____

II. COMMENTS

Because of the limitations of space in this manual, the comments of these analysis lessons will be kept brief.

1. The description of 1:7-8, showing the cities and land of Judah as laid waste and burned, could be history as well as prophecy. If the devastations and sieges by Syrians (under King Rezin), Israelites (under King Pekah), Edomites, and Philistines had already come (2 Chron. 28), then Isaiah may have been referring to these. The larger and more significant intent of his words, however, was the prediction of utter desolation yet to come—a prophecy fulfilled in 701 B.C. when the Assyrian forces under Sennacherib came against Jerusalem.

2. Read 1:13b thus: "As for the festival of the new moon and the sabbath (and) the convoking of a convocation—I cannot stand iniquity and (i.e., along with) a solemn meeting."[1]

1. Charles F. Pfeiffer and Everett F. Harrison, eds., *The Wycliffe Bible Commentary* (Chicago: Moody, 1962), p. 610.

The appointed feasts (v. 14) were probably the three main annual feasts: Passover and Unleavened Bread (first month); Pentecost (third month); and Tabernacles (seventh month).

3. The reference to sins "as scarlet" (v. 18) is a vivid picture of the indelible quality of the crimson dye that came from the scarlet worm.

4. The conditional prophecy of 1:20 was fulfilled in Sennacherib's invasion of 701 B.C. and the Chaldean invasion of 586 B.C.

5. Concerning the title "Holy One of Israel," Gleason Archer writes:

> This name for God is the most significant title employed by the prophet Isaiah. In chapter 6 Jehovah reveals himself in a scene of heavenly glory as the Holy One (**Qadosh**), i.e., the transcendent God, who is wholly separate from the frailty and finiteness of Creation (his majesty-holiness), and wholly separate from the sinfulness and defilement of man (his purity-holiness). But this Holy One has claimed the family of Abraham, Isaac, and Jacob as his covenant children. He has given himself to them, and they have given themselves to him in a covenant undertaken nationally on their part and solemnized before Mount Sinai (Ex. 19:5-8). Therefore he is the Holy One of Israel.[2]

III. SUMMARY

The first chapter of Isaiah reveals the various feelings and reactions of the Lord that were brought on by the sins of His chosen people. Their unfaithfulness hurt Him; their hypocritical worship angered Him; and their apostasy distressed Him. He pronounced severe judgment for all these sins, but in tenderness and compassion He also offered hope of deliverance, cleansing, and restoration to any who would obey Him, even though they would be a small minority, "a very small remnant."

2. Ibid., p. 609.

Lesson 6

Isaiah's Call and Commission

God's call to Isaiah for a prophetic ministry came in the year when one of Judah's better kings, Uzziah, died. Things were looking dark for Judah at that time: spiritually, the nation's heart was hardened; and politically, foreign powers were beginning to threaten annihilation of the land and people. This was the ripe hour for God to send forth a man as His mouthpiece to tell the world that He was still the God of history and that He still wanted to be enthroned in the hearts of His creatures.

When Isaiah wrote his book, he apparently had a reason for not recording the testimony of his call at the beginning of the book. A look at the outline of the first large division, chapters 1–12, may suggest why.

ISAIAH 1—12   **Chart K**

PROPHECIES OF JUDAH			
1 2	6	7	12
INTRO- DUCTION BOOK OF HARDENING	ISAIAH'S CALL	BOOK OF IMMANUEL	

Chapter 1 is an appropriate introductory chapter to the eleven chapters that follow, because it gives the general picture of Judah's relation to God. There were estrangement, and so judgment (amplified in the Book of Hardening, chaps. 2–5); and there was a coming Saviour, and so hope (prophesied in the Book of Immanuel, chaps. 7–12). Isaiah was called to deliver both messages,

51

and the record of his call was placed between both books—Hardening and Immanuel.

I. ANALYSIS

Read the chapter several times in the course of your study, using a modern version. Try to picture the scene and the action, and try to hear the voices of the speakers. Make a note of strong words and phrases appearing throughout the chapter. Write a list of things you are seeing for the first time. Note any verses that are difficult to understand.

Note by Chart L how this segment may be divided into four paragraphs. Record short paragraph titles on your own analytical chart.

Where in the chapter does the call actually begin? Note how this is shown on the chart by the outline in the narrow vertical column: SETTING; CALL.

_____

_____

What spiritual lesson about divine call is suggested by this?

_____

What is the main point of each paragraph? What is the atmosphere of each of the first two paragraphs?

_____

_____

Compare the ending of the chapter ("holy seed") with the opening verses ("holy, holy, holy")

_____

_____

Now study each paragraph individually, using the following study suggestions. Try to record your answers on the analytical chart.
1. Read verses 1-4. Who is the central person here?

_____

_____

SETTING	1 SIX WINGS Lord Seraphim	SETTING Glorification
REACTION	5 LIVE COAL Woe is me . . . thine iniquity is taken away	Confession
CALL **RESPONSE** **COMMISSION**	8 HERE AM I Lord—Who will go for us? I—Here am I; send me He—go and tell	CALL Lord's Question
EXPLANATION	11 HOW LONG? I—Lord, how long? He—Until . . . 13	Isaiah's Question

Observe the various things that point to him as such. Why did the seraphim *cover* their faces and feet?

_____

_____

Analyze carefully this ascription:

> *"Holy, holy holy,* is the Lord of *hosts:*
>
> *the whole earth* is full of his *glory"* (v. 3).

2. Did Isaiah actually see God? (Cf. John 1:18.) Read John 12:37-41 for help in answering this. Note especially verse 41 and the word "glory."

_____

_____

3. Where were the throne and the temple of verse 1?

_____

_____

4. Read verses 5-7. Account for Isaiah's reaction. Note that Isaiah identified himself with his people, sinful as they were.

_____

How did he identify God?

_____

5. What was the purging agent of verses 6-7? (Read Num. 31:22-23; Mal. 3:2; Matt. 3:11.) It is of interest to note that the root of the word "seraphim"[1] is *saraph,* meaning "fiery."

_____

6. Read verses 8-10. According to the wording of verse 8, was the call a general one or made only to Isaiah?

_____

_____

---

1. The word "seraphim" in the Bible appears only in this chapter.

Observe the simplicity of the conversation:
  "Whom shall I send?"
  "Here am I; send me."
  "Go, and tell."
Write out some important truths taught by these lines.

_____

_____

_____

_____

7. Study the picture:
   greasy ("fat") hearts
   heavy ears
   sticky ("shut") eyes
How does each phrase describe the spiritual condition of the people of Judah?

_____

_____

_____

8. Verses 9 and 10 read as though Isaiah's ministry was to keep people from turning to God. Why are the words of the commission put in the imperative form? Read Jesus' application of these words in Matthew 13:13-17. Observe especially the phrase "their eyes *they* have closed" (v. 15).

_____

_____

9. Read verses 11-13. The previous paragraph opened with the Lord's question. Now Isaiah asked a question. What may Isaiah have had in mind when he asked this question?

_____

Observe in this paragraph the twofold message of judgment and salvation. Read verse 13 thus: "And if there be yet a tenth in it, it also shall in turn be eaten up: as a terebinth, and as an oak, whose stock remaineth, when they are felled; so the holy seed is the stock thereof" (ASV*). "Stock" ("substance," King James Version) refers to the stump of the tree, from which shoots would later appear. How was this prophetic of salvation for a remnant?

_____

*American Standard Version.

10. Write out some lessons taught by this chapter about:
DIVINE CALL

_____

_____

LORD'S GLORY

_____

_____

CONFESSION OF SIN

_____

_____

CHRISTIAN SERVICE

_____

_____

HARDENED HEARTS

_____

_____

II. COMMENTS

At the beginning of his public prophetic ministry Isaiah was given a spiritual experience of divine ordination that he would never forget. Surely he, like the apostle Paul, shared his testimony about this with his audiences from time to time.

It was important for Isaiah to have an indelible vision of the Lord in all of His holiness, for Isaiah was to preach to people of unclean lips and hardened hearts. Also the vision would enhance his ministry to kings on earthly thrones, for he would see "the King" (6:5) sitting upon the heavenly throne, "high and lifted up" (6:1) above all kings. Isaiah lived to see five different kings reigning over Judah, and the responsibility resting upon his shoulders to be a spokesman for God to them was always heavy.

Isaiah was accustomed to hearing many different sounds filling the air in the Temple at Jerusalem. When he was transported to the heavenly temple, however, he heard one prominent song, the song of the fiery attendants (seraphim) ascribing holiness and glory to the Lord of hosts. When he saw and heard of the glory of the Lord, he looked within his own heart and saw the ugliness and corruption of his sin. And when this was purged by the fiery coal from the altar of incense, then he was spiritually prepared to hear the Lord's call for his lifework. Christians seeking God's will concerning their future would do well to learn from Isaiah's experience. With a cleansed heart the believer is given a keen sense of hearing the voice of the Lord as He reveals His will.

Answering God's call should be as simple as the call itself. In the call God did not give extra details, such as how many witnesses He wanted or how He would send them out. It was simply, "Whom shall I send, and who will go for us?" Isaiah's response was likewise simple, without conditions or questions, 'Here am I; send me." When the commitment was made, *then* God gave further details (vv. 9-10) and *then* Isaiah asked a question (v. 11).

Isaiah's commission was for a lifetime. He was to preach and keep on preaching, for the people needed to hear God's message until the consummation of judgment. There would never be a ceasing of the witness of God's word, and out of the hosts that would hear a remnant would continue, as "holy seed" of God.

III. SUMMARY

As a summary exercise reread this chapter, and list the various things taught about the prophet and his prophetic office.

Lesson 7

Isaiah 52:13–53:12

The Suffering Servant

Isaiah is called the evangelical prophet because he says so much about the coming Messiah and His gospel. Of the many messianic passages in Isaiah, the one we shall study in this lesson is considered the preeminent one. It has been called Isaiah's "golden passional." G. Campbell Morgan says of the prophecy, "There is nothing, either in the Old or the New Testament, more arresting than this portrayal of the Servant of the Lord, in which we are conscious of an appalling gloom, which nevertheless burns and shines with ineffable glory."[1]

The many details of Christ's death and exaltation prophesied by Isaiah in this passage remind one of King David's messianic Psalm 22 written three centuries earlier. The minute details of prophecy already fulfilled in Christ are irrefutable evidence of the miraculous inspiration of Scripture. Liberal theologians, and even orthodox Jews, continue to deny that Jesus is the servant of Isaiah 53. But the New Testament identification is clear. Read the story of Philip and the Ethiopian eunuch (Acts 8:26-38) and also these other New Testament quotes:

Isaiah	Quoted in New Testament
52:15	Rom. 15:21
53:1	John 12:38; Rom. 10:16
53:4	Matt. 8:17
53:5-6	1 Peter 2:22-25
53:7-8	Acts 8:32-33
53:12	Mark 15:28; Luke 22:37

1. G. Campbell Morgan, *Great Chapters of the Bible* (New York: Revell, 1935), p. 104.

Before analyzing the "Suffering Servant" passage, review your survey study that shows the context of this prophecy. Chart M is an excerpt from the survey chart.

ISAIAH 40—66   **Chart M**

COMFORT OF GOD		
40	49	58 66
TRUE GOD	SUFFERING MESSIAH	REIGNING LORD
Redemption Promised	Redemption Provided	Redemption Realized

```
            52:13—53:12
            BEHOLD
            MY SERVANT
```

This messianic passage, a key to the doctrine of the comfort of God, is located in the center of the second division of Isaiah's book called Comfort of God. The slain Lamb of God, about which the passage speaks, is the clue to peace with God. Recall from Chart I that whereas "throne" is a key subject of chapters 1–39, "lamb" is a key subject of chapters 40–66. Revelation 7:17 brings both of these together, showing how God's comfort comes from them: "For *the Lamb which is in the midst of the throne* shall feed them, and shall lead them unto living fountains of waters: and God shall *wipe away all tears* from their eyes." It is interesting to observe that two key words in the book of Revelation, a book that speaks mostly of end times, are "Lamb" and "throne." The former appears twenty-nine times and the latter forty times in the book.

I. ANALYSIS

Read the passage carefully and prayerfully. Always keep in mind that the ultimate purpose of all Bible study, regardless of methods used, is to *let the Bible do something to you*. Have an open heart and a sensitive spirit throughout your study.

As you prepare to analyze, mark off paragraph divisions in your Bible according to those shown on Chart N. Notice that each paragraph is three verses long. Record paragraph titles.

(1) EXALTED

52:13	Exalted
15	

(2) SMITTEN

LIFE

53:1	Despised

—the despised Man

SUFFERING

4	Wounded

—the vicarious Sufferer

DEATH

7	Cut off

—the atoning Lamb

(3) REWARDED

10	Divide a portion
12	

What were your impressions after the first reading?

_____

_____

_____

Write a list of key words and phrases for this passage.

_____

_____

_____

If some of the verses are familiar because you had already memorized them, do not let this keep you from analyzing carefully every verse, familiar or not.
What is the main point of each paragraph?

_____

_____

_____

Record an outline of the passage on your analytical chart. Observe any similarities of the first and last paragraphs. How are the three middle paragraphs different from each other?

_____

_____

_____

1. Read 52:13-15. In what way is Christ exalted now?

_____

_____

How will He be exalted in the future?

_____

_____

Notice the comparison: "[Just] as many were astonished...so shall he sprinkle [or startle]..." (vv. 14-15). What is the point here? Read Romans 15:21 for a fulfillment of the last part of verse 15.

2. Read 53:1-3. For the meaning of verse 1, read John 12:38-41 and Romans 10:16. Note that the key word of 53:1 is "believed." How does the verse relate to the last verses of chapter 52?

In what ways did Jesus' life and ministry fulfill the prophetic description of verses 2 and 3?

3. Read 53:4-6. Observe the frequency of the word "our." The *Berkeley Version* translates 5b thus: "The punishment which procured our peace fell upon Him." What are the various descriptions of the sinner in the paragraph?

Note also the phrase "for our," speaking of Christ's vicarious, or substitutionary, work.
4. Read 53:7-9. Study the descriptions of Jesus' trial, death, and burial. Observe how specific the prophecies are (e.g., "grave ... with the rich in his death;" cf. Matt. 27:57-60).
5. Read 53:10-12. What is the atmosphere of this paragraph?

Notice all the bright words (e.g., "satisfied"). What different things are prophesied about Christ here?

How is this paragraph a fitting conclusion to the passage 52:13–53:12?

6. As a concluding exercise reread the entire passage and note all the references to mankind. As you read, identify yourself as a member of the sinful human race, and you will be impressed all the more how merciful and gracious God is to provide such salvation for you.

II. COMMENTS

For Christ, the way to the crown was the cross. His exaltation could only follow His humiliation. The apostle Paul wrote this inspired interpretation of Jesus' ministry:

> Christ Jesus . . . although He existed in the form of God, did not regard equality with God a thing to be grasped, but emptied Himself, taking the form of a bondservant, and being made in the likeness of men. And being found in appearance as a man, He humbled Himself by becoming obedient to the point of death, even death on a cross. Therefore also God highly exalted Him, and bestowed on Him the name which is above every name, that at the name of Jesus every knee should bow, of those who are in heaven, and on earth, and under the earth, and that every tongue should confess that Jesus Christ is Lord, to the glory of God the Father (Phil. 2:5-11, NASB*).

Another prominent truth of Isaiah 52:13–53:12 is the substitutionary sacrifice of Christ. Christ died *in the place of* sinners. He died "for our transgressions," "for our iniquities" (v. 5). This truth is clearly taught in the New Testament (read such passages as 1 Cor. 15:3; 2 Cor. 5:21; Rom. 5:8.; 1 Peter 2:24; 3:18; John 10:11; Mark 10:45). The penalty of sin is death, and Christ as vicar, or substitute, died in the place of the sinner. Isaiah says, "The Lord hath laid on him the iniquity of us all" (53:6). Of the phrase "hath laid on him" *The Wycliffe Bible Commentary* makes this literal translation: *"caused to alight upon him,* or better still, *caused to meet him."* The commentary makes this observation: "Cf. Num. 35:19, where the revenger of blood is authorized to slay the murderer when he 'meeteth' him in the way—the same verb being used there as here. Our transgressions were to 'meet' him in the way and slay him as if he were the guilty one instead of us."[2]

The description of Jesus as having "no beauty that we should desire him" (53:2) perplexes many readers. The physical appearance of Jesus is not intended here, rather His personality. But did He not have a compassion for others that would have been recognized by the words He spoke and by the things He did—and which would have been told by even His very eyes and facial movements? The answer is that Jesus' personality was beautiful, but sinful man's eyes were blind to that beauty. His beauty was God's beauty, not man's. People watched Him perform miracles,

---

*New American Standard Bible.
2. Charles F. Pfeiffer and Everett F. Harrison, eds., *The Wycliffe Bible Commentary* (Chicago: Moody, 1962), p. 647.

but they saw no glamour. They looked for regal splendor and saw only a Man of humble circumstances. They thought He should act like a king triumphantly marching to claim a throne; instead they saw Him put on a cross. Isaiah's description emphasizes *what people saw in Jesus* ("when we shall see him," 53:2), and what they saw made them hide their faces from Him. Isaiah is thus describing the *appearance* of Jesus and the *nature* of man's sinful heart. To this day sinful men persistently avoid "facing the real Christ, preferring a 'historical Jesus,' who would not trouble them with his cross."[3]

III. SUMMARY

Four words serve to summarize this masterpiece of messianic prophecy:
> SERVICE ("Behold, my servant," 52:13)
> SORROW ("Man of sorrows," 53:3)
> SACRIFICE ("Pierced for our transgressions," 53:5, *Berkeley*)
> SEED ("He shall see his seed," 53:10)

Here is the heart of the gospel, its profound words including so much doctrine that Dwight L. Moody referred to it as his creed "already in print."

3. Ibid.

Lesson 8
The Man Jeremiah

About sixty years after Isaiah's death, God called Jeremiah, a young man of approximately twenty-one, to the difficult but urgent task of proclaiming His word to Judah on the eve of judgment. The dark clouds hanging over nations of the world today for idolatrous and apostate hearts remind one of the spiritual conditions that faced Jeremiah then. History is our teacher here, and that is why the study of the book of Jeremiah promises to be such a profitable one. F. Cawley has said, "The discovery of the real Jeremiah may well be the rebirth of the discoverer."[1]

Before we look at the book itself, let us follow the pattern established earlier in the manual, that of first becoming acquainted with the prophet who wrote the book.

I. HIS NAME

The name Jeremiah translates the Hebrew word *yirme-yahu*, to which has been assigned the literal meaning "Jehovah throws." On the basis of this, various translations have been made, such as "Jehovah establishes," "Jehovah exalts," "Jehovah is high," and "whom Jehovah appoints." Any of these names would have been appropriate for the prophet called to such a ministry as his.

II. HIS RANK AMONG THE PROPHETS

Someone has said of Jeremiah, "Amid all the bright stars of Old Testament history there is not a name that shines brighter than that of Jeremiah." By divine design it was Jeremiah who was called to prophesy in the darkest hours of Judah, when Judah as a nation

---

1. F. Davidson, ed., *The New Bible Commentary* (Grand Rapids: Eerdmans, 1953), p. 609.

died. He is known as the "weeping prophet" and "the prophet of the broken heart." But he wept not for his own trials, grievous as they were. It was the sins of his nation and the fearful destruction those sins were bringing upon them that broke Jeremiah's heart. Jeremiah lived in a day when tragic events were unfolding, and he, as perhaps no one else at the time, comprehended their full significance. He knew that within a short time the proud, beautiful city of Jerusalem with its magnificent Temple would be in ruins and that his beloved people would be in captivity. He also knew that the nation that had been God's own peculiar treasure would be set aside for a time because of incorrigibility and that supremacy would be given to the Gentiles. No wonder Jeremiah wept. "Who can watch unmoved, even at a distance of twenty-five hundred years, the death agony of a nation, and that nation the chosen people of God?"

Of all the writing prophets, Jeremiah and Isaiah stand out preeminently. To place one above the other is perhaps arbitrary, for in many ways their ministries were different and therefore difficult to compare. Their personalities differed, Isaiah being the bold and fearless type, Jeremiah the gentle and compassionate. Isaiah lived more than one hundred years before the captivity of Judah; Jeremiah ministered just before and during the final catastrophe. (See Chart X). Isaiah had *foretold* the judgments that were coming unless the nation turned to God; Jeremiah's particular mission to Judah toward the end of his career was to notify the nation that their judgment *was at hand*, that God had rejected them (at least for the present), and that nothing now could save them from the punishment they so deserved.

Chart O shows other prophets who ministered during Jeremiah's time. You may want to refer to a Bible dictionary for a brief description of each of these as background to your study of Jeremiah. The prophets are: Nahum, Zephaniah, Habakkuk, Daniel, and Ezekiel. They were all faithful spokesmen for God; Jeremiah was prince among them.

III. TIMES IN WHICH HE LIVED

When one reads the history of the times in which Jeremiah lived (read 2 Kings 22–25), he does not wonder that God would no longer bear with His people. Through Isaiah, God had said all He could say to keep them back from ruin, and they heeded not. So when Isaiah's voice was still, there was virtual silence on the part of God for about fifty years. During that time He spoke no word to the nation by the mouth of a prophet, as though He would stand aside and see if His very silence would cause them to think of

66

Him. But the nation continued hard and fast on their headlong plunge to destruction. Look at Chart X and observe the absence of a prophet during the reign of King Manasseh.

Scarcely had Isaiah and good King Hezekiah been laid to rest when idolatry and numberless heathen abominations began to flourish in the land under the reign of Manasseh, one of the worst kings Judah ever had. Whatever he could do to provoke the Lord to wrath he did. One of the most daring of his sins was to desecrate the court of the Temple by building altars to Baal and to set up a graven image in the holy house where God had set His name. (Read 2 Kings 21.)

The moral condition of Judah in the days of Jeremiah is pungently described by the prophet in 5:31: "The prophets prophesy falsely, and the priests bear rule by their means; and my people love to have it so." For fifty years blasphemous insults to God were heaped up by king, priest, and people, until the climax was reached and Judah's doom was irrevocably sealed. Although the judgment was postponed for a while because of the tender heart and righteous life of King Josiah, twenty-five years after his death the kingdom of Judah was a thing of the past.

Into this political and moral turmoil God sent Jeremiah to be His spokesman.

It is never an easy task to carry God's Word to an obstinate, erring people, bent on having their own way. At a time like this, the time of the end for Judah, when political affairs were at fever heat and religious conditions were utterly corrupt, the prophet's task was an exceedingly difficult one.

Much of Jeremiah's ministry concerned the international situation in which Judah was intimately and precariously involved. Look at Chart U and observe that Canaan was the geographical link between Egypt in the southwest and Syria, Assyria, Babylon, and other nations in the north. Each nation sought to be *the* world power. Control of Canaan was a must for such a claim.

Study Chart O for orientation in the historical setting of Jeremiah.

Observe the three groups of contemporaries:

1. *Contemporary prophets.* These have been referred to above.

2. *Contemporary kings.* These are the kings who were reigning over Judah while Jeremiah prophesied. Only Josiah was a good king. Jehoahaz and Jehoiachin reigned for only a brief time. Josiah, Jehoiakim, and Zedekiah were the kings that played a major role in Jeremiah's career. Sections of the book of Jeremiah referring to these reigns are:

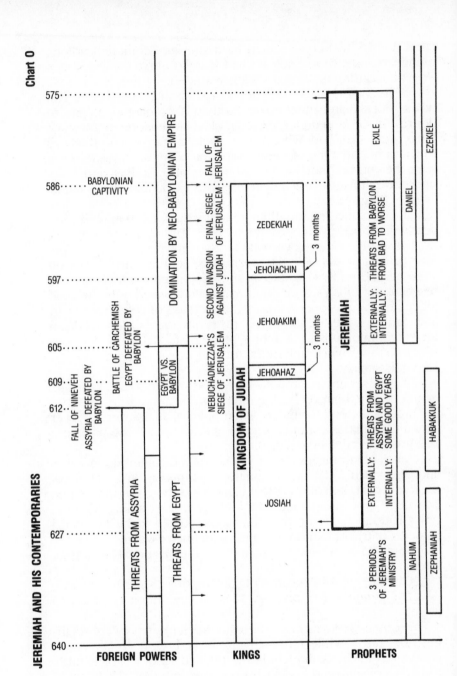

Chart O

JEREMIAH AND HIS CONTEMPORARIES

575
586 ..... BABYLONIAN CAPTIVITY
597
605
609
612
627
640

FOREIGN POWERS

FALL OF NINEVEH
ASSYRIA DEFEATED BY BABYLON
BATTLE OF CARCHEMISH
EGYPT DEFEATED BY BABYLON
EGYPT VS. BABYLON

THREATS FROM ASSYRIA

THREATS FROM EGYPT

DOMINATION BY NEO-BABYLONIAN EMPIRE

FALL OF JERUSALEM
FINAL SIEGE OF JERUSALEM
SECOND INVASION AGAINST JUDAH
NEBUCHADNEZZAR'S SIEGE OF JERUSALEM

KINGS

KINGDOM OF JUDAH

ZEDEKIAH
JEHOIACHIN — 3 months
JEHOIAKIM
JEHOAHAZ — 3 months
JOSIAH

PROPHETS

JEREMIAH

EXILE
THREATS FROM BABYLON
EXTERNALLY: THREATS FROM BAD TO WORSE
INTERNALLY:

EXTERNALLY: THREATS FROM ASSYRIA AND EGYPT
INTERNALLY: SOME GOOD YEARS

3 PERIODS OF JEREMIAH'S MINISTRY

EZEKIEL
DANIEL
HABAKKUK
ZEPHANIAH
NAHUM

68

Josiah: 2:1–12:17
Jehoiakim: 13:1–20:18; 25:1–27:11
Zedekiah: 21:1–24:10; 27:12–39:18

It would be helpful for you in your study to refer to an outside source for descriptions of these kings of Judah to whom Jeremiah spoke God's counsel.

3. *Contemporary foreign powers.* Observe that in the early part of Jeremiah's ministry, Judah was threatened mainly by Egypt and Assyria. Judah was continually tempted to make an alliance with one power so as to be protected from the other. Jeremiah's consistent message was to get right with God and trust *Him* for protection from any nation.

In the latter part of Jeremiah's career, the threats were from Babylon. Two events had brought about the change of threat: (1) the Assyrians were defeated by the Babylonians in 612 B.C. with the fall of Nineveh; (2) the Egyptians were defeated by the Babylonians in 605 B.C., at the Battle of Carchemish. Judah resisted Babylon, but Jeremiah, by direction from God, urged Judah to give in to Babylon so as to avoid *utter destruction*, since the divine judgment of captivity was inevitable.

The various prophecies of Jeremiah spoken at different times in his ministry are more understandable when this international setting is kept in mind.

IV. HIS CHARACTER

Jeremiah is an example of one whose divine commission hardly matched his personality, as human reasoning would compare the two. In the words of John Graybill, Jeremiah was

> afraid of people's "faces," one whom we should consider singularly unfitted for the work placed upon him. That he tenaciously clung to his assigned task through the succeeding years of rejection and persecution is a tribute both to the mettle of the man and to the grace of God, without which his personality surely would have gone to pieces.[2]

Though Jeremiah was timid by nature, he was given a bold message to proclaim—and he proclaimed it. Though he was sensitive, his task was to pronounce drastic and extreme judgment. He was sympathetic and loyal to his fellowmen, but these qualities

2. Charles F. Pfeiffer and Everett F. Harrison, eds., *The Wycliffe Bible Commentary* (Chicago: Moody, 1962), p. 656.

did not surpass his loyalty to God and his love for God's righteousness. His faith in God bolstered all that he said or did, and his great courage endured only because he patiently rested in the wisdom of God's timetable. Jeremiah was truly a saint of God whose example all of us would do well to follow.

V. HIS PERSONAL HISTORY

From the Bible we learn more about Jeremiah's life than we do about Isaiah's. Many practical lessons can be gleaned from the book of Jeremiah about the demanding task of being a witness for God to an unsympathetic and rebellious audience.

Jeremiah was born when wicked King Manasseh was still ruling over Judah. He was raised in a small town called Anathoth, located just a few miles north of Jerusalem. His father was a priest, Hilkiah by name (other Bible references to Hilkiah are not to this man). Following in the footsteps of his father, Jeremiah entered the priesthood at an early age. When he was still a young man, probably around twenty-one, God made known to him that he had been divinely ordained to be a prophet and that his duties as priest were terminated (chap. 1).

Jeremiah immediately embarked on his new course and for about fifty years stood as the representative and spokesman for God. Jeremiah had a trying life, more so than any of the other prophets. His message was such as to provoke opposition from his nation. Kings, rulers, priests, and politicians, as well as the false prophets, vehemently opposed the policy that Jeremiah recommended to the nation, and in order to silence him they brought all manner of persecution against him.

Jeremiah has recorded for us some of the trying experiences he endured, when he was ridiculed, ignored, beaten, misrepresented, starved, mocked, threatened, and cursed by all classes of people, even by those whom he had considered his friends.

1. Read Jeremiah 11:18-23 and 12:6, and try to imagine how he must have felt when he discovered that his own neighbors and kinsfolk were plotting against his life.

2. Read 18:11-18, and see how the people would "smite him with the tongue" and ignore his words as he stood in the streets of Jerusalem and preached the word of God to them.

3. Read 26:1-15, and see how he was treated when he preached in the courts of the Temple. The priests and false prophets joined with the people to arrest and threaten with death this faithful servant of God.

4. Read 32:1-3; 38:6-13, 28, and see how he was imprisoned and subjected to hardship.

These and numberless other persecutions Jeremiah endured. But more agonizing than all else must have been the pain of knowing that the work that cost him so much would not swerve the nation one hair's breadth from the downward course on which it was determined to proceed. True, God had told him that part of his ministry would be "to build, and to plant" (1:10), but the weeping prophet knew that this referred only to a small remnant.

Jeremiah's life was one long, sad, stormy day. Often he grew discouraged and was almost ready to give up the battle, but the fire of the Spirit in his bones kept him true to God (read 20:9). In the words of James Gray,

> God placed him between two "cannots" or, if you please, between two fires. There was the fire of persecution without, and that of the Holy Spirit within, the latter being the hotter of the two. To avoid being consumed by the one, he was more than willing to walk through the other. "I cannot speak any more in God's name," he says at one time, and follows it by adding, "I cannot refrain from speaking."[3]

Jeremiah's personal life was lonely. We have noted above that even his friends and relatives plotted to kill him. He was instructed of God not to marry and raise a family (16:1-4). But he had one companion at his side throughout most of his career: Baruch. Baruch served as Jeremiah's secretary, playing an important part in the story of the scrolls of the prophet's messages (Jer. 36:4ff.). Chapter 45 is devoted wholly to a message from God to him. Baruch remained close to Jeremiah throughout all the stormy years, and the two went into exile together.

In 605 B.C., after Jeremiah had been preaching for twenty-two years, the Chaldean army under Nebuchadnezzar swept down from the northeast and carried away to Babylon King Jehoiakim and other leaders of Judah, along with the costly vessels of the Temple. Daniel, who was then only a youth, was among those taken (2 Chron. 36:2-7; Jer. 45:1; Dan. 1:1-3). The people of Judah, proud and stubborn as ever, refused to be warned by this judgment and, in spite of Jeremiah's pleading, continued in their course of sin.

After eight years the king of Babylon again invaded Judah, this time carrying away thousands of the inhabitants as captives. (Read 2 Kings 24:10-17, cf. Jer. 52:28-30. Consult a commentary for an explanation of the numbers listed.) This second warning proved

---

3. James M. Gray, *Synthetic Bible Studies* (New York: Revell, 1923), p. 148.

as ineffectual as the first, and about ten years later the same enemy came down for the final blow. With an immense army Nebuchadnezzar surrounded Jerusalem (to which city most of the Jews from the smaller towns had fled) and prepared for a prolonged siege. For eighteen months the Jews withstood the siege and refused to surrender. During this time, Jeremiah was constantly urging his people to surrender, declaring that there was no hope of victory, that God's set purpose was to chastise them for their sins by captivity in Babylon. Jeremiah's preaching so angered the king of Judah, Zedekiah, that he imprisoned and starved the prophet nearly to death, but he could not silence him. When the Jews were finally compelled to surrender, the king of Babylon burst into the city and did his worst. Not content with surrender, he went through the streets burning, murdering, and torturing. He killed the king's sons and put out the king's eyes. This is described in 2 Chronicles 36:17-21.

But amid all the tumult of falling walls and burning city, God remembered His servant Jeremiah. Not only was Jeremiah preserved from all harm, but the Chaldeans treated him with the utmost kindness as a reward for the policy of nonresistance that he had sponsored. They offered him the choice of either going to Babylon with his people or staying in his own land with the few poor Jews who were allowed to live there under the rule of a Chaldean governor. Jeremiah chose to remain in the land where God had placed His people (see Jer. 39:10-14; 40:2-6).

After the Chaldean armies had withdrawn, Jeremiah pleaded with the Jews who remained to turn from their sin to God. But they ignored his advice, murdered the Chaldean governor, and then fled into Egypt against the counsel of Jeremiah, who told them this was against God's will. Jeremiah was compelled to go with them, and in the last chapters of his book we read the messages that he spoke to them in Egypt (chaps. 40–45). To the very end of his long ministry this prophet of "the bleeding heart and iron will" solemnly and bravely warned and pleaded with his beloved but erring people. Defiant and impertinent as ever, they ignored and insulted him.

The Bible gives no details of Jeremiah's death. One tradition says that he was stoned to death in Egypt by the very Jews he tried so hard to save.

VI. HIS CALL

Jeremiah must have received his call to the prophetic office when he was a mere youth. His call was much more commonplace than

72

that of Isaiah (cf. Isa. 6). Jeremiah saw no dazzling vision, no throne or seraphim. Quietly the Lord spoke to the youth, setting before him his difficult task and promising to be with him through every experience.

Read Jeremiah 1:4-10, and notice the following points regarding his call:

1. It was prenatal (vv. 4-5).
2. He shrank from the work because of his youth and inexperience (v. 6).
3. He was not excused from service (v. 7).
4. God assured him of divine guardianship (v. 8).
5. He received the personal touch of God and His divine message (v. 9).

Jeremiah's ministry was to be both constructive and destructive. Mostly he would be a prophet of judgment and for this would receive constant opposition from kings, princes, priests, false prophets, and others. Jeremiah naturally shrank from both the difficulties and the responsibilities of the work assigned him. But he counted on God's promise to be with him (1:8, 19), and when he stood before the people he never quailed. God so sustained him and made His presence such a reality that Jeremiah dared anything in his public capacity.

VII. HIS MESSAGE

We have seen some things about the *man* Jeremiah. Now let us look at his *message* (content) and the *method* by which he delivered that message.

A. Content

Chapter 1, which we shall study more closely in Lesson 10, identifies Jeremiah's message as twofold: (1) "to destroy" (Destruction) and (2) "to build" (Construction). When identified more specifically, there were four parts to his message, as shown in Chart P.

Jeremiah's ministry concentrated mainly on the first two themes, a message that understandably was unpopular. He was sent to Judah to rebuke them for their sinful ways. He was to announce that because of their ways Jehovah had rejected them for the present and that it was His purpose to transfer earthly dominion (which He had promised to this chosen nation on condition of obedience) into the hands of the Gentiles. God had borne with Judah long and patiently, but the limit of endurance had been reached. The time had come for God to withdraw His protection

	Four Themes	Emphasis	Time element
DESTRUCTION	1. Rebuke	People's sin	Present condition (cf. 2:1-37)
	2. Warning	God's righteousness	Future predicted (cf. 20:4; chaps. 23-26, 31)
CONSTRUCTION	3. Invitation	God's grace	Present offer (cf. 3:1—4:4)
	4 Consolation	People's hope	Future predicted (cf. 23:1-40; 30:4-11; 32:37-41; 33:14-26)

from the nation and allow their enemies to come in and do their worst.

It is interesting to observe that Jeremiah's message was not really new. Even Moses, a thousand years earlier, had foretold the kind of judgment that would come for rebellion against God (read Lev. 26:27-39; Deut. 28).

The false prophets were Jeremiah's bitterest enemies. They claimed to have communication from Jehovah but were teaching exactly opposite to Jeremiah. The false prophets ridiculed his teaching and advised an alliance with other nations for the purpose of resistance, claiming that God had promised victory.

However, Jeremiah did not only preach judgment. Often he voiced God's invitation to return to Him: "Return, thou backsliding Israel, saith the Lord; and I will not cause mine anger to fall upon you" (3:12). That was his message of conditional immediate restoration. He also spoke of the more distant future, prophesying preservation of a remnant, the initiating of a new covenant, and the coming of a Saviour. Though he did not prophesy as much as Isaiah did on this subject, his prophecies were just as strong and clear. (Read such passages as 23:5-6; 31:31-34; 32:37-41).

B. Method

Jeremiah usually introduced his message with a phrase such as "The word of the Lord came to me, saying" (e.g., 2:1). Sometimes that message came to Jeremiah by way of a vision (e.g., "What seest thou?" 1:11, 13), which the prophet would then share with his people. On occasion Jeremiah was given an experience that was intended to symbolize a spiritual truth, and he would pass this on to his audience. In Lesson 11 we will be studying the symbol of potter and clay as that parable is given in chapter 18. Other similar experiences of Jeremiah involved these object lessons: marred girdle (chap. 13); full bottle (chap. 13); drought (chap. 14); broken bottle (chap. 19); two baskets of figs (chap. 24); bonds and bars (chap. 27); purchase of a field (chap. 32); hidden stones (chap. 43). You will find all of these stories interesting and instructive reading.

Jeremiah often cited history to illustrate his point. His messages were also filled with constructive teaching of the major doctrines pertinent to the life of the Jews of his day.

It is not an exaggeration to say that Jeremiah was a master teacher and preacher. He did not convert Judah, because what he had to say fell on spiritually deaf ears. "His loftiest counsels were ignored, his writings torn to shreds by a tyrant king, his name blackened, his life hunted, and his worst predictions horribly fulfilled before his tear-filled eyes."[4] According to earthly standards, such a career is measured as a failure. But in the eyes of God, who in commissioning Jeremiah foretold that his audience would fight against him (1:19), the prophet's mission was a success.

1. By what title is the man Jeremiah known?

_____

2. In what respect was Jeremiah a contrast to the prophet Isaiah?

_____

_____

3. Study briefly the moral and religious condition of Judah at the time Jeremiah prophesied.

_____

_____

4. Compare Jeremiah's call with that of Isaiah.

_____

_____

_____

4. John Phillips, *Exploring the Scriptures* (Chicago: Moody, 1965), p. 144.

5. What were the main points of Jeremiah's message to the nation?

_____

_____

_____

_____

_____

6. Why did Jeremiah counsel Judah to surrender to Babylon?

_____

_____

_____

7. Recall the highlights of Jeremiah's personal history.

_____

_____

_____

_____

_____

8. Describe the character of Jeremiah.

_____

_____

_____

_____

_____

9. About how old was Jeremiah when he was called to be a prophet?

_____

When he died?

_____

Lesson 9
The Book of Jeremiah

Jeremiah's message is particularly relevant for today because of the many similarities to our times. These are days of idolatry, hypocrisy, rebellion, and apostasy; relationships between world powers are strained and precarious; the Jews have a vital part in writing history; God's prophets are in a minority; and judgment seems near. Jeremiah has something to say about all of these. W.W. White called Jeremiah "the bravest, grandest man of Old Testament history." The prophet's book is a challenge to all serious Bible students.

I. COMPOSITION OF THE BOOK

Though the theme of divine judgment for sin runs throughout the book of Jeremiah, the organization of the materials of the book is not always clear. From the record itself we learn that Jeremiah wrote the different parts, including biography, history, doctrine, and prediction, at various times and under diverse circumstances. When all the parts were brought together on one scroll as one book, a general pattern of composition was followed, placing the discourses in the first half of the book and reserving the latter half mainly for narrative. Jeremiah appropriately used the story of his call and commission as the introduction of the book, and supplements were added at the end. Here is the general pattern of the entire book:

1	2	21	34	45	52
INTRO. CALL	DISCOURSES	SPECIAL PROPHECIES	NARRATIVE	SUPPLEMENTS	

By its very nature such a pattern does not call for a strict chronological sequence. It is clear that Jeremiah's approach was primarily topical, not chronological.[1] At the same time it may also be said there is a *general* chronological progression in the order of Jeremiah's discourses. Refer to Chart Q and note the order of kings: Josiah, Jehoiakim, Zedekiah.

There is an underlying topical progression in the book of Jeremiah. The climax is the fall of Jerusalem, which is recorded at two places toward the end of the book. All that goes before, which includes mainly Jeremiah's discourses and personal experiences, points to that hour of tragedy.

II. SURVEY OF THE BOOK OF JEREMIAH

We come now to the "skyscraper view" of Jeremiah's book. The first thing to do is to make a brief scanning of the entire book, chapter by chapter, observing what the general contents of each chapter are. Record a chapter title for each chapter on a chart similar to Chart Q.

In this first reading exercise, identify the various *groups* of chapters with similar content. These are as follows:

Content

Chapters
  2–20: Series of prophecies of doom
  21–29: Nebuchadnezzar appears throughout this section
  30–33: The bright prophecies concerning the new covenant
  34–39: Account of the siege and fall of Jerusalem
  40–44: After the fall of Jerusalem
  46–51: Prophecies concerning the foreign nations

This should be your starting point in making an outline for the book. Note that most of the book of Jeremiah is represented by the above groups. You will want to go back to some of the chapters and look at them more closely. Try to make your own outlines of the book; then compare them with the outlines shown on Chart Q.

1. That historical chronology is not observed can be seen by the references to the kings. The order of the kings of this period is, as we know, Josiah, Jehoahaz, Jehoiakim, Jehoiachin, and Zedekiah. (See 1:1-3. Also refer to Chart O.) For example, observe that 21:1 sets the time of that discourse when Zedekiah was reigning; 25:1 goes back to the fourth year of Jehoiakim; 26:1 and 27:1 to the beginning of the reign of this king; 28:1 refers again to the time of Zedekiah. In reading the book, keep this in mind.

Chart Q

SURVEY CHART OF JEREMIAH
JEREMIAH BOOK OF JUDGMENT

A key verse: 1:10

	BOOK I		BOOK II			SUPPLEMENTS
	MAINLY ORACLES	ORACLES AND NARRATIVE	MAINLY NARRATIVE			MAINLY ORACLES
INTRODUCTION	DISCOURSES	SPECIAL PROPHECIES	NARRATIVE			THREE SUPPLEMENTS

KEY EVENT: FALL OF JERUSALEM

1	2	11	21	30	34	40	45	46	52
CALL	PUBLIC SERMONS	PERSONAL EXPERIENCES	CERTAINTY OF CAPTIVITY	BOOK OF CONSOLATION	SIEGE AND FALL OF JERUSALEM	AFTER THE FALL	BARUCH	FOREIGN NATIONS	FALL OF JERUSALEM

Josiah and Jehoiakim	Zedekiah mainly (Jehoiakim insertions)	Jehoiakim and Zedekiah

79

Observe the following concerning this survey outline.

1. The main body of the prophecy is made up of chapters 1-44. Chapters 45-52 compose three supplements.

2. The main body is divided into two parts: Book I and Book II. The division is made at chapter 21, because (1) at this point historical narrative begins to play an important part in the prophecy, and (2) these chapters refer mostly to the time of King Zedekiah, whereas the previous chapters refer to the reigns of Josiah and Jehoiakim.

3. There are three groups of discourses in which Jeremiah denounced sin, urged repentance, and warned of judgment to come:

Public Sermons (chaps. 2–10)
Personal Experiences (chaps. 11–20)
Certainty of Captivity (chaps. 21–29)

4. The brightest section of the book is that of chapters 30–33, known as the Book of Consolation. Here Jeremiah looks beyond the years of captivity and sees a restoration; and he looks beyond the age of the old covenant and sees the new (cf. 31:31). It is noteworthy that this bright prophecy appears in the text just before Jeremiah narrates the siege and fall of Jerusalem. Compare this with the locations of *songs* throughout the book of Revelation just before the descriptions of judgments.

5. Chapters 34–44 are mainly narrative, recording the key event of the book—the fall of Jerusalem—and the events preceding and following it. In chapters 40–44 two interesting observations may be made: (1) Jeremiah was just as faithful to God and to the Jews after the judgment fell as he was before, and (2) the Jews remained just as stubborn and impenitent as ever.

6. Observe the contents of each of the three supplements. Why would each of these be placed at the end of the book? Concerning the oracles against the foreign nations, it should be observed that God judges all nations alike on the issue of sin. For example, though God used Babylon as His agent of punishment against the Jews, Babylon was not spared judgment for its own sin (read 50:14).

7. In your study of this book look for a key verse that adequately represents the theme of the book. There are many possibilities (e.g., 1:10).

8. Many verses scattered throughout the book might be classified as golden texts. Be on the lookout for these, and make a note of them as you read them. Here is a suggested list: 6:16; 9:23-24; 10:10-13; 17:7-10; 18:4-6; 20:9; 22:29; 23:5-6.

9. The title Book of Judgment has been assigned Jeremiah's prophecy because this represents the prominent theme of his discourses and also because the climax of the narrative is the judgment of Judah's fall.

Jeremiah, living in the last days of the surviving kingdom of Judah, was a prophet of judgment. From the people's standpoint his discourses were extremely disagreeable and irritating. In the first place, the people were deeply in love with sin, which they determined not to renounce. It was exceedingly unpleasant for them to be confronted on the street corner, in the Temple, in their homes, anywhere and at any time, and have their unfaithfulness to God described in the plainest kind of language (such as 3:1-2, which no doubt they designated as vulgar) and to have their pet idols ridiculed (10:2-5), their mock pity exposed (7:1-20), and their political policy attacked. It was not agreeable to them to be continually urged to repent and be saved. They did not like to listen to Jeremiah's lamentations and gloomy predictions. Jeremiah was, therefore, an unpopular preacher. They thought he was an extreme pessimist. We can imagine the people's contrasting him with some of the false prophets. Instead of a mournful countenance and solemn warnings, these false prophets met the people with a smile and a word of cheer. "Peace, peace!" said the false prophets. But there was no peace. "There is no peace, saith my God, to the wicked." No wonder the people listened to the false prophets and spurned Jeremiah. But the grim reality was that destruction was knocking at the door, as Jeremiah was preaching.

III. SYMBOLS OF JEREMIAH

As mentioned in Lesson 8, many symbols appear in the book of Jeremiah. The main ones involved Jeremiah's actual experiences, where God was teaching him, and thus Judah, some vital spiritual truths. Here are some of the prominent ones (read the passages):

A. The Linen Girdle (13:1-11)

God showed Jeremiah, under the figure of the linen girdle, how He had purchased Israel that they might cleave to Him and live for His praise and glory, as a beautiful girdle might bring forth praise for a person wearing it. But Israel's pride and self-will were so great that they would have to be sent to Babylon and kept there until they could learn that they were in themselves like the girdle that was marred: good for nothing.

81

B. The Potter and the Clay (18:1-8)

Here God taught the further truth that even though the nation was "marred" in the hands of the potter, yet He, the divine Potter, could still make it a glorious vessel fit for His use.

C. The Shattered Vessel (19:1-13)

Irrevocable judgment was taught by the action of this symbol: "Even so will I break this people and this city, as one breaketh a potter's vessel, that cannot be made whole again" (v. 11). This did not contradict the promise of the restoration of a remnant.

D. Celibacy of Jeremiah (16:1-9)

By commanding Jeremiah not to marry and raise a family, God was showing something of the utter woes of the coming judgment, affecting not only the men and armies but mothers and children as well.

E. Field of Anathoth (32:6-44)

In order to reiterate His promise that the Jews would return to the land after the term of captivity had ended ("houses and fields and vineyards shall be possessed again in this land," v. 15), God instructed Jeremiah to purchase a plot of land in his hometown of Anathoth. It was a most unlikely time for such a transaction (Jeremiah was in prison, and the enemy was besieging the city), but this only served to emphasize the intention of the symbol. Did Jeremiah *really* believe the message of restoration he was prophesying? When the prophet balked (vv. 17-25), God countered with the challenge, "Is there anything too hard for me?" (v. 27). We do well to learn from this experience of Jeremiah.

IV. CONFESSIONS OF JEREMIAH

Jeremiah's humble and contrite spirit often brought forth confessions of sin. Study the following passages, and list some important lessons to be learned from these confessions (the passages marked with an asterisk are recommended for analysis using the analytical chart method):

10:23-24

_____

11:18–12:6*

_____

15:10-21*

_____

17:9-11, 14-18

_____

18:18-23

_____

20:7-18

_____

V. JEREMIAH AND END TIMES

Jeremiah, like his predecessor Isaiah, foretold the sure restoration of God's people to their land. But passages like Jeremiah 30:3; 31:8-30, 31-37; 32:36-44; 33:6-18 indicate that the return from Babylon at the end of the seventy years was not considered as a complete fulfillment of these prophecies. The prophet had a great restoration in view, a fuller and more complete fulfillment of the prophecies. In the above passages both Israel and Judah are mentioned as returning. The gathering is spoken of as being not only from Babylon but from all nations of the earth. Also references to the new covenant, great prosperity and blessing, and deep penitence and obedience of the people speak of a still future time.

What is the basis for such bright hope for God's people in the end times, when the history of the Jews throughout the centuries since the nation's birth has been so dark? God Himself has already answered this question in one of the chapters about the new covenant:

Yea, I have loved thee with an everlasting love: Therefore with lovingkindness have I drawn thee. Again I will build thee, and thou shalt be built, O virgin of Israel. (31:3-4)

Israel has a future, spoken of by Paul in Romans 11, only because of the unchangeable, unfathomable, eternal love of God.

1. Does the book of Jeremiah follow a topical or chronological order, mainly?

_____

Identify, by the names of kings, the book's general chronological order.

_____

_____

_____

2. Review Chart Q, and then try to reproduce it without any further help.

3. What is the main historical event in Jeremiah?

_____

_____

How is the book organized around it?

_____

_____

4. Where is Jeremiah's call recorded?

_____

Compare this with that of Isaiah.

_____

_____

5. Why were Jeremiah's discourses so particularly disagreeable to the people of Judah?

_____

6. Why would God chastise the nations that He had used to chastise Judah?

_____

84

7. Name and describe some of the symbols of Jeremiah's experiences.

_____

_____

_____

_____

_____

8. In predicting the Jews' return from captivity, did Jeremiah and Isaiah have in view a greater restoration and a more complete fulfillment of the prophecies?

_____

Explain.

_____

9. On the basis of your survey study, list some evidences of God's love and mercy in the book of Jeremiah.

_____

_____

10. List other important spiritual truths you have already learned in Jeremiah.

_____

_____

_____

_____

_____

Lesson 10

Jeremiah 1:4-19

Jeremiah's
Call and Commission

The successful career of any man of God doing God's work is attributable to his ordination and sanctification by God for this work, before he was even born. This is what the priest Jeremiah heard one day from God concerning his own life, and with this assuring commission he embarked on his stormy but successful prophetical course. Jeremiah's testimony about this, recorded in the first chapter of his book, has been a blessing and a challenge to God's people throughout all the centuries since he wrote it down. Let us study this passage with prayerful diligence, that we too may be blessed thereby.

I. ANALYSIS OF 1:4-19

Read chapter 1 at least once before you begin to record anything, in order to get the feel of the passage. Keep a mental note of impressions during this reading. The first three verses of chapter 1 are introductory to the entire book of Jeremiah and will not be studied as part of this segment. However, the identification of Jeremiah as a priest when the Lord spoke to him is pertinent to his commission as a prophet.

Before reading the segment 1:4-19 again, mark off in your Bible the following paragraph divisions: at verses 4, 9, 11, 13, and 17. Keep these paragraph units in mind as you read. The paragraphical method of study is profitable in studying the book of Jeremiah. The writer's commentary *Jeremiah: Prophet of Judgment*[1] may be consulted for further help in studying Jeremiah in this manner.

Underline key words and phrases in your Bible. Note especially *repeated words and related* phrases. Record observations on paper. Begin to organize your observations to derive outlines and

1. Irving L. Jensen, *Jeremiah: Prophet of Judgment* (Chicago: Moody, 1966).

86

PROPHET UNTO NATIONS
JEREMIAH 1:4-19

① PROPHET BY SOVEREIGN APPOINTMENT

Before: Priest (v. 1)

Now: Prophet

4

I knew thee
I formed thee
I sanctified thee
I ordained thee

GO

9

SPEAK

My words in thy mouth

② PROPHET WITH A SOVEREIGN MESSAGE

11

rod of an almond tree

"What seest thou?"

13

seething pot

③ PROPHET UNDER SOVEREIGN PROTECTION

17

My fortifications about thee

19

87

theme. Record your studies on an analytical chart similar to Chart R. The studies on Chart R are examples of the kinds of observations you want to make yourself. Do your own independent study before looking at the chart too closely.

1. Note the two visions which were part of Jeremiah's experience. Translate 12*b* as "for I watch over my word to perform it" (ASV). What was the point of each vision? Record on the analytical chart.
2. Observe how verse 17 continues the formal commission of verses 5-10.
3. How much did Jeremiah speak on this occasion?

_____

_____

What may be learned from this?

_____

_____

What was the content of what he said?

_____

_____

What is known of Jeremiah from this?

_____

_____

4. Read verses 4-8 again. Analyze verse 5 carefully. Observe the set of four divine activities, in the past tense. List important truths taught by this.

_____

_____

Note that God did not say anything about speaking here, yet Jeremiah's first response was "I cannot speak." Relate that response to the word "prophet" at the end of verse 5. What does this reveal about Jeremiah's understanding of what the prophet's task basically was?

_____

_____

Note all the other references to *speaking* in verses 4:19. Study the contrasts of verses 6-8. Note especially:
   "I cannot speak" (v. 6).
   "Thou shalt speak" (v. 7).

5. Read verses 9 and 10. Pause over the tremendous implications of the phrase "my words in thy mouth" (v. 9). What was Jeremiah's twofold mission, according to verse 10?

_____

What six figures are listed in verse 10?

_____

How many refer to the one phase of his work and how many to the other?

_____

What does this suggest as to emphasis?

_____

_____

6. What sins are cited in verse 16?

_____

7. Read verses 17-19. What commands were given Jeremiah?

_____

What predictions of opposition to Jeremiah did the Lord speak?

_____

What assurances were given?

_____

_____

8. Go over this passage a few more times, looking for more nuggets of truth. Close scrutiny is always rewarded by new discoveries. When you have completed your study, write a list of spiritual lessons that you have learned from this passage.

_____

_____

_____

_____

_____

II. COMMENTS

Prophets of God learned of their commission only by special divine calling. This was different from the office of the priest, for a man could become a priest by birth, as son of a priest. Jeremiah was priest by birth and prophet by divine calling. (Note: It should be recognized that divine predestination was operative not only for the prophets but also for the men who were priests of God by family inheritance, for their birth "location" was in the divine plan.)

Jeremiah's reticence in responding to God's call was based on his inability to speak, for, said he, "I am a child" (1:6). The word translated "child" is *na'ar*, which could refer to any age up to about forty-five. (Joshua was a *na'ar* at forty-five, cf. Ex. 33:11). Jeremiah was only a young man in his early twenties at that time, but his objection "I am a child" probably referred more to the weaknesses and inabilities that he himself recognized would hinder such a public ministry.

The vision of the almond tree shoot ("rod," King James Version) in verses 11 and 12 is an example of a play on words. The text reads: "Jeremiah, what seest thou? And I said, I se a rod [shoot] of an almond tree [Hebrew, *shaked*, awake]. Then said the Lord unto me, Thou hast well seen: for I will hasten [*shoqed*, watch over] my word to perform it." "The connection of the vision and the application may be seen in the fact that the almond tree, blossoming around January, was the first tree to awaken from the long winter's night, its blossoms appearing before the leaves. The symbol of awakeness befitted God's Word, for though His people had settled into a dark, cold sleep of spiritual dearth, His Word was ever awake, watched over by Him, bringing about its daily unalterable fulfillment of sovereign design."[2]

The vision of the seething pot ("boiling caldron," ASV) showed Jeremiah the main judgment facing Judah: conquerors from the north coming upon Jerusalem and other cities of Judah and laying them waste. When this vision came to Jeremiah, Assyria was the great world empire, but God had Babylon in mind (cf. 25:9 and chap. 39). Though Babylon was located east of Judah, any army of Babylon coming upon Judah would do so from the north, because of the impassable Arabian desert.

II. SUMMARY

This passage of Jeremiah's call and commission teaches clearly that the main task of a prophet was to speak for God. It was God who would bring down judgment upon the people of Judah for their sin; and it was God who would spare a remnant. But God wanted a man to warn Judah of those judgments and to console the faithful few for their faith.

2. Ibid., pp. 20-21.

God did not have to search for such a man. He was on hand by predetermined design, serving among the priests of Anathoth. Now the hour for his call had arrived, and God sent the word that moved him to the office of prophet. When Jeremiah accepted the commission, he was thrust forth with an indelible impression of sovereign appointment, sovereign message, and sovereign protection.

Lesson 11

Jeremiah 18:1-23

The Parable of the Potter

The long-suffering of God and the faithful service of His prophet Jeremiah to stubborn sinful people are the lessons of the parable of the potter.

The parable is one of the more familiar ones of the Old Testament. Its lessons are timeless and universal. Refer to Chart Q, and note that this chapter is in the section called Personal Experiences, toward the end of Book I. The action took place during Jehoiakim's reign, with more than ten years to go before Judah's fall. Keep this in mind as you study the chapter.

I. ANALYSIS OF 18:1-23

Paragraph divisions for this segment should be made at verses 1, 5, 12, 18, and 19. Follow the reading and analysis procedure of the previous lessons in your study of this passage. Record all impressions, observations, and questions. Chart S will suggest some studies to be pursued further, and it will also furnish some clues as to the organization of the chapter. Try to originate as many studies as you can before referring to outside helps. Record these on your analytical chart. The following study questions will suggest items to be recorded.

1. What is the main point of each paragraph? Study the outline in the right-hand margin.

_____

_____

2. Note on Chart S how the segment may be divided into three parts, thus:

92

GOD'S OFFER TO REMAKE ISRAEL
JEREMIAH 18:1-23

Chart S

LONG-SUFFERING OF GOD	1 Potter's house	the symbol
	5 So are ye	the message
REFUSAL OF ISRAEL	12 Horrible	the response and consequences
INVOLVEMENT OF JEREMIAH	18 Devices	the prophet's involvement
	19 Forgive not 23	the prophet's plea

93

Long-suffering of God
Refusal of Israel
Involvement of Jeremiah

In your own words, what does the passage teach about each of these subjects?

_____

_____

_____

_____

3. What is the one main teaching of the parable (vv. 1-4)? What are the other related teachings in the parable?

_____

_____

4. Was the Israel of verse 6, as clay in the potter's hand, already marred when God spoke the words? Use verses 7 and 8 to guide you in your answer.

_____

_____

5. How big was Israel's sin of verse 12? Note the repetition of the strong phrase "we will." Study God's commentary on that sin, as He speaks in verses 13-16.

_____

_____

6. Why did Israel heap its wrath upon Jeremiah (v. 18)? (Note: Reference to "the prophet" is to the false prophet, whom Israel was heeding.)

_____

_____

7. What is the basis for Jeremiah's imprecatory prayer of the last paragraph?

_____

_____

8. Read Romans 9:20-24 for some related truths derived from the figure of the potter and his clay.

9. List some of the main spiritual lessons taught by this chapter.

_____

_____

_____

_____

_____

_____

II. COMMENTS

The scene of a potter forming an object out of clay was a familiar one in Jeremiah's day. The wheels were two circular stones connected by a vertical shaft. The lower wheel was turned by the feet, engaging the upper wheel to its circular motion. The potter thus had two free hands to form the vessel from the lump of clay. It was easily within his power to remake the marred vessel, as long as the clay was still pliable enough to be molded. Israel, by continual refusal of God, kept getting harder and harder in heart, till eventually God could not mold the clay.

The passage 18:7-9 is a key passage on the conditional character of prophecy. Observe the words "if" and "repent" in these verses. On the meaning of divine "repentance," *The Wycliffe Bible Commentary* says,

> The use of the word **repent** in referring to God does not imply fickleness on the part of the Almighty. When a human word is used to describe the actions of the Divine, the word undergoes a subtle redefinition. God is not a man that he should repent (cf. 4:28; 15:5)—he does not blow hot and cold. Yet he does **relent** when his people turn to him; and this action of relenting is called **repentance** (cf. 20:16; 26:3, 13, 19; 42:10).[1]

This parable of the potter is followed in Jeremiah by another parable concerning pottery: the parable of the broken earthen bottle, recorded in 19:1–20:6. Its lesson is an extension of the earlier parable, the two being compared thus:

1. Charles F. Pfeiffer and Everett F. Harrison, eds., *The Wycliffe Bible Commentary* (Chicago: Moody, 1962), p. 671.

The Marred Vessel: teaching the sovereignty and long-suffering of God; the invitation of a second chance, and its rejection and consequence.

The Broken Bottle: teaching the awfulness and irreversibility of the impending judgment.

III. SUMMARY

> Behold, as the clay is in the potter's hand, so are ye in mind hand, O house of Israel. (18:6)

The parable of the potter, simple though it is, illustrates some of the Bible's greatest doctrines. Included among these are:

The almightiness of God: potter as compared with the clay

The sovereign authority of God: potter controlling the clay

The long-suffering of God: potter offering to remake the vessel

The love of God: potter wanting to make a good vessel

Lesson 12
The Book of Lamentations

Lamentations is an appropriate sequel to the prophecy of Jeremiah, for it looks back to the same event that Jeremiah anticipated: the fall of Jerusalem, 586 B.C.

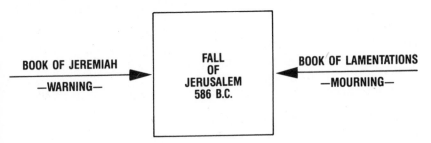

BOOK OF JEREMIAH	FALL OF JERUSALEM 586 B.C.	BOOK OF LAMENTATIONS
—WARNING—		—MOURNING—

Knowing from his prophecies how Jeremiah wept over his people before judgment fell, it is not difficult for us to imagine the depths to which his soul sank in grief as he watched the holy city burning and his people being ravished. Lamentations reveals something of the pathos of that experience.

I. TITLE

Two of the most common titles assigned to this book in Hebrew Bibles are:

 1. *Ekhah* ("Ah, how," or "Alas"), the opening word of chapters 1, 2, and 4. Note how the word is translated in your English Bible at these places.

 2. *Qinoth* ("Lamentations," or "Elegies"), a title representing the content of the book and the melancholy meter of its five poems.

The *qinoth* title was retained in the Greek Bibles, with the Greek translation *Threnoi* ("lamentations," from *theomai*, "to cry aloud"). This was carried over into the Latin Bibles as *Liber Threnorum* ("Book of Lamentations") and thence into the English Bibles as *Lamentations*.

II. PLACE IN THE BIBLE

In the threefold Hebrew Bible (Law, Prophets, Writings), Lamentations appears in the last part, in a section called Megilloth. The Megilloth is a group of five Old Testament books that the Jews read publicly on national holidays. Lamentations is read on the ninth day of Ab (about mid-July), the anniversary of the destruction of Jerusalem in 586 B.C. and A.D. 70.

In our English Bible, Lamentations appropriately follows the book of Jeremiah. The translators of the Greek Septuagint (100 B.C.), recognizing its Jeremianic authorship, also placed it here.

III. AUTHOR

Though other authors are suggested (e.g., Baruch), the evidence points strongly to Jeremiah. Some of this evidence is listed here:

1. The Septuagint introduction to the book: "Jeremiah sat weeping and lamented with this lamentation over Jerusalem, and said . . . "

2. Hebrew and Gentile tradition.

3. Similarities between Lamentations and poetical portions of Jeremiah (cf. also 2 Chron. 35:25).

4. The writer, an eyewitness of Jerusalem's destruction, had a sensitivity of soul and ability to write.

IV. COMPOSITION AND STYLE

Lamentations is a set of five elegies (melancholy poems), the first four of which follow an acrostic pattern (first letter of lines, or groups of lines, representing each of the twenty-two letters of the Hebrew alphabet).

The poetic meter is described as a limping meter, having three beats in the first line trailing away in a mourning two-beat line. When publicly read, the chanting gave support to the mood of the words.

Many poetic styles and devices appear in these poems. Vivid imagery is perhaps the most prominent one.

V. MESSAGE

The message of Lamentations is threefold:
1. *Mourning over Jerusalem's judgment for sin.* Most of the book presents this. Compare Jesus' mourning over Jerusalem in Luke 13:34-35 and 19:41-44.
2. *Confession of sin* (e.g., 1:8; 3:59; 5:16).
3. *Ray of hope* (e.g., 3:21-32; 5:21). Only one who saw into the far-distant future could speak of hope. Babylon was the conqueror now and Jerusalem the vanquished; in that future day, it would be glory for Jerusalem and desolation for Babylon. With such a hope, Jeremiah could exclaim, "Great is thy faithfulness" (3:23*b*).

VI. ANALYSIS

Read through the book of Lamentations in one sitting, observing moods, emphases, key thoughts, and other large items.

Then study each poem individually, recording your observations as you study. Try to discover the following for each poem:

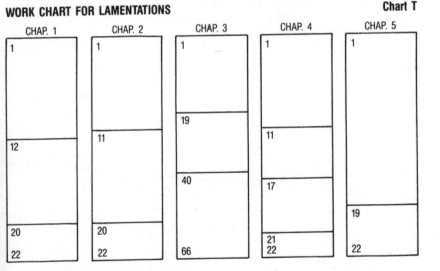

WORK CHART FOR LAMENTATIONS — Chart T

1. The main theme of the poem
2. Groups of subjects within each poem (stanza divisions shown in Chart T are from ASV)
3. References to sin
4. Rays of hope
5. Prayers (note that all of chap. 5 is a prayer)

99

As a concluding step in your study, write a list of vital spiritual lessons taught by Lamentations. How applicable are these to today?

_____

_____

_____

_____

_____

A FINAL NOTE

You have now concluded your study of two great prophets of God—Isaiah and Jeremiah. You have learned about the men themselves, their Lord, their message, and the people to whom they ministered.

Today this world is engulfed in moral and spiritual darkness that is blacker than that of the prophet's time. There is only One who can conquer that darkness—Jesus, the light of the world. Pray that God will raise up more prophets like Isaiah and Jeremiah who will heed His call to proclaim Jesus.

Would *you* answer such a call?

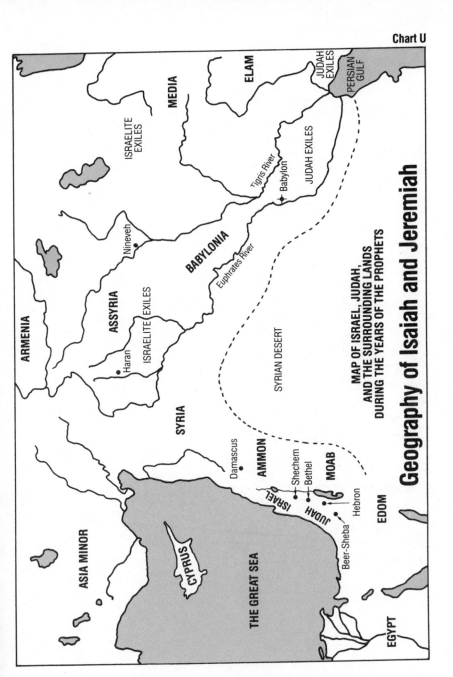

Geography of Isaiah and Jeremiah

MAP OF ISRAEL, JUDAH, AND THE SURROUNDING LANDS DURING THE YEARS OF THE PROPHETS

KINGS OF ISRAEL

Chart V

Kings of Israel	Character	Relations with Judah	Relations with Other Countries	History
1 JEROBOAM	bad	war		1 Kings 11:26—14:20 2 Chron. 9:29—13:22
2 NADAB	bad	war		1 Kings 15:25-28
3 BAASHA	bad	war		1 Kings 15:27—16:7 2 Chron. 6:1-6
4 ELAH	drunkard	war		1 Kings 16:8-10
5 ZIMRI	murderer	war	war with Philistines	1 Kings 16:10-20
6 OMRI	very bad	war		1 Kings 16:16-27
7 AHAB	exceedingly wicked	alliance	war with Syria	1 Kings 16:28—22:40 2 Chron. 18
8 AHAZIAH	bad	peace		1 Kings 22:40, 51-53 2 Kings 1:1-17 2 Chron. 20:35-37
9 JORAM	bad	alliance	war with Moab war with Syria	2 Kings 3:1-3; 9:14-25 2 Chron. 22:5-7
10 JEHU	bad	war		2 Kings 9—10 2 Chron. 22:7-12
11 JEHOAHAZ	bad	peace		2 Kings 13:1-9
12 JEHOASH	bad	war		2 Kings 13:10-25; 14:8-16 2 Chron. 25:17-24
13 JEROBOAM II	bad	peace		2 Kings 14:23-29
14 ZECHARIAH	bad	peace		2 Kings 15:8-12
15 SHALLUM	bad	peace		2 Kings 15:13-15
16 MENAHEM	bad	peace		2 Kings 15:16-22
17 PEKAHIAH	bad	peace		2 Kings 15:23-26
18 PEKAH	bad	war	war with Assyria first captivity	2 Kings 15:27-31 2 Chron. 28:5-8
19 HOSHEA	bad	peace	conquered and carried away captive by Assyria	2 Kings 17:1-41

KINGS OF JUDAH

Kings of Judah	Character	Relations with Israel	Relations with Other Countries	History
1 REHOBOAM	bad	war	invasion of Egypt	1 Kings 12-14 2 Chron. 10-12
2 ABIJAM	bad	war		1 Kings 15:1-8 2 Chron. 13:1-22
3 ASA	good	war	league with Syria	1 Kings 15:9-24 2 Chron. 14:1—16:14
4 JEHOSHAPHAT	good	peace		1 Kings 22:41-50 2 Chron. 17-20
5 JEHORAM	bad	peace	war with Edom	2 Kings 8:16-24 2 Chron. 21
6 AHAZIAH	bad	alliance	war with Syria	2 Kings 8:25-29; 9:27-29 2 Chron. 22:1-9
7 ATHALIAH (queen)	bad	peace		2 Kings 8:18, 25-28; 11:1-20 2 Chron. 22:1—23:21; 24:7
8 JOASH	good	peace	threatened by Syria	2 Kings 11:1—12:21 2 Chron. 22:10—24:27
9 AMAZIAH	good	war	war with Edom	2 Kings 14:1-14 2 Chron. 25
10 UZZIAH	good	peace		2 Kings 15:1-7 2 Chron. 26
11 JOTHAM	good	war	war with Syria	2 Kings 15:32-38 2 Chron. 27
12 AHAZ	bad	war	war with Syria alliance with Assyria	2 Kings 16 2 Chron. 28
13 HEZEKIAH	good		war with Philistines and Assyrians	2 Kings 18-20 2 Chron. 29-32
14 MANASSEH	bad			2 Kings 21:1-18 2 Chron. 33:1-20
15 AMON	bad			2 Kings 21:19-23 2 Chron. 33:21-25
16 JOSIAH	good			2 Kings 22:1—23:30 2 Chron. 34-35
17 JEHOAHAZ	bad		war with Egypt	2 Kings 23:31-33 2 Chron. 36:1-4
18 JEHOIAKIM	bad		tributary to Egypt first deportation	2 Kings 23:34—24:5 2 Chron. 36:5-7
19 JEHOIACHIN	bad		war with Babylon second deportation	2 Kings 24:6-16 2 Chron. 36:8-10
20 ZEDEKIAH	bad		war with Babylon final deportation	2 Kings 24:17—25:7 2 Chron. 36:11-21

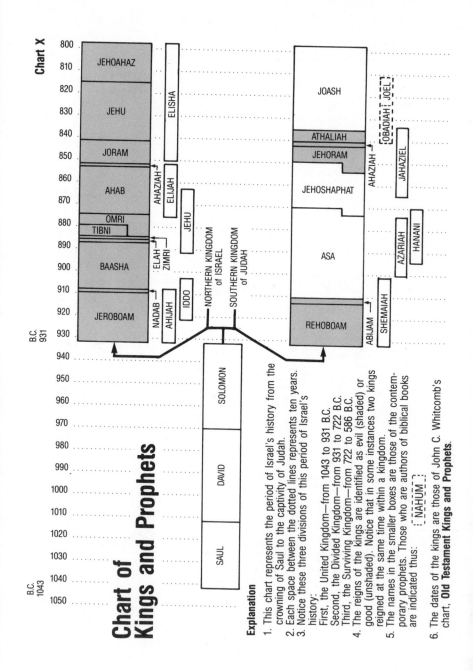

Chart of Kings and Prophets

Explanation

1. This chart represents the period of Israel's history from the crowning of Saul to the captivity of Judah.
2. Each space between the dotted lines represents ten years.
3. Notice these three divisions of this period of Israel's history:
   First, the United Kingdom—from 1043 to 931 B.C.
   Second, the Divided Kingdom—from 931 to 722 B.C.
   Third, the Surviving Kingdom—from 722 to 586 B.C.
4. The reigns of the kings are identified as evil (shaded) or good (unshaded). Notice that in some instances two kings reigned at the same time within a kingdom.
5. The names in the smaller boxes are those of the contemporary prophets. Those who are authors of biblical books are indicated thus: ⌐ NAHUM ¬
6. The dates of the kings are those of John C. Whitcomb's chart, **Old Testament Kings and Prophets**.

104

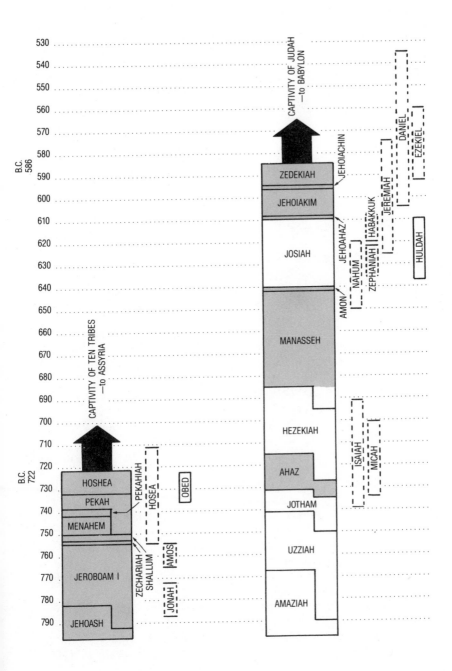

Bibliography

COMMENTARIES AND TOPICAL STUDIES

COMMENTARIES ON ISAIAH

Archer, Gleason L. "Isaiah." In *The Wycliffe Bible Commentary*, ed. Charles F. Pfeiffer and Everett F. Harrison. Chicago: Moody, 1953.

Fitch, W. "Isaiah." In *The New Bible Commentary*, ed. F. Davidson. Grand Rapids: Eerdmans, 1953.

Ironside, Henry A. *Expository Notes on the Prophet Isaiah*. New York: Loizeaux, 1952.

Kelly, William. *An Exposition of the Book of Isaiah*. Minneapolis: Klock and Klock, 1979.

Martin, Alfred, and John Martin. *Isaiah: The Glory of the Messiah*. Chicago: Moody, 1983.

Young, Edward J. *Studies in Isaiah*. Grand Rapids: Eerdmans, 1954.

COMMENTARIES ON JEREMIAH AND LAMENTATIONS

Cawley, F. "Jeremiah." In *The New Bible Commentary*, ed. F. Davidson. Grand Rapids: Eerdmans, 1953.

Davidson, Robert. *Jeremiah and Lamentations*. Philadelphia: Westminster, 1986.

Erdman, Charles R. *The Book of Jeremiah and Lamentations*. Westwood, N.J.: Revell, 1955.

Feinberg, Charles. *Jeremiah, A Commentary*. Grand Rapids: Zondervan, 1982.

Graybill, John F. "Jeremiah." In *The Wycliffe Bible Commentary*, ed. Charles F. Pfeiffer and Everett F. Harrison. Chicago: Mooyd, 1962.

106

Jensen, Irving L. *Jeremiah and Lamentations.* Everyman's Bible
 Commentary. Chicago: Moody, 1956.
Kaiser, Walter. *A Biblical Approach to Personal Suffering.* Chicago:
 Moody, 1982.
Price, Ross. "Lamentations." In *The Wycliffe Bible Commentary*,
 ed. Charles F. Pfeiffer and Everett F. Harrison. Chicago:
 Moody, 1962.

RESOURCES FOR FURTHER STUDY

Archer, Gleason L. *A Survey of Old Testament Introduction.* Chica-
 go: Moody, 1964.
Bullock, C. Hassell. *An Introduction to the Old Testament Prophet-
 ic Books.* Chicago: Moody, 1986.
Jensen, Irving L. *Jensen's Survey of the Old Testament.* Chicago:
 Moody, 1978.
New International Version Study Bible. Grand Rapids: Zondervan,
 1985.
Ryrie Study Bible (NIV). Chicago: Moody, 1986.
Sauer, Erich. *The Dawn of World Redemption.* Grand Rapids:
 Eerdmans, 1953.
Strong, James. *The Exhaustive Concordance of the Bible.* New
 York: Abingdon, 1890.
Unger, Merrill F., ed. *New Unger's Bible Dictionary.* Chicago:
 Moody, 1988.